Kyoto University African Study Series 028

Cultural tourism potentials towards livelihood security
Local perceptions in Southern Ethiopia

Azeb Girmai

©2021 Azeb Girmai
Printed in Japan
Shoukadoh Book Sellers

Center for African Area Studies, Kyoto University
Yoshida-Shimoadachi-cho 46, Sakyo, Kyoto 606-8501

First Published 2021 by Shoukadoh Book Sellers

Library of Congress Cataloguing-in-Publication-Data

Azeb Girmai
Cultural tourism potentials towards livelihood security: Local perceptions in
Southern Ethiopia

ISBN978-4-87974-765-5

This book was published with the Grant for Young Researchers of the FY
2020.
Discretionary Budget of the President of Kyoto University.

Acknowledgements

I would like to express my sincere acknowledgement and gratitude to all who have made it possible for me to complete my doctoral thesis. It would have not been easy if not for all the guidance, inspiration, and emotional support I received from them.

I am indebted to those who trusted me and shared their information and reflections at both of my research sites: My host families and support, those who took the courageous task of being photographers and video film makers, and all who participated in the research in Jinka, South Ari, and Mursiland, Salamago Woredas. Special thanks to Elfenesh Kibo, Mamush Mixa, Narugo Chagnoyeale, Natuye Birabi, Bardole Gnarabiand, Oli Jarholi Birabi, Dozer Charneli Olibui, Nashne Logologny, and Namargo Oligidani.

I am grateful for all the support I received from the Japan Student Services Organization (JASSO) "Monbukagakusho Honors Scholarship for Privately Financed International Students" and Japan Educational Exchange Services (JEES), to accomplish this research and learn a great deal, as well as the Center for On-Site Education and Research at Kyoto University (Explorer program) for sponsoring my doctoral field research.

My special thanks go to the Culture and Tourism Office in Jinka, South Omo Zone, and the South Omo Research Center and staff; Tesfaye Abate from the Pioneer Zonal Guide Association and his family; Daniel Galshi from the *Akimi Ye Negew Sew Guide Association*; Mamo Mala from the South Omo Development Association; and Professor Gebre Yintiso, Dr Dikaso Unbushe, Ato Argachew Bochena, and all the staff at Jinka University for their kind support and assistance.

Finally, I would like to express my sincere gratitude and thanks to my academic supervisors Professor Masayoshi Shigeta, Professor Takahashi Motoki, and Assistant Professor Kaneko Morie for their unflagging guidance and support.

Finally, I owe a great debt to my entire family—my husband Dawit Dejene, our son Yohannes Dawit, and our daughter Elilta Dawit. I could not have done this without your full support. Finally, I offer my thanks to the Lord God for enabling me to start and finish it.

CONTENTS

LIST OF TABLES

LIST OF FIGURES

LIST OF PHOTOS

LIST OF ANNEX

LIST OF ABBREVIATIONS

ETB	Ethiopian Birr
ESTMP	Ethiopian Sustainable Tourism Master Plan
FGD	Focus Group Discussion
GDP	Gross Domestic Product
GTP II	Growth and Transformation Plan II
MCT	Ministry of Culture and Tourism
SLF	Sustainable Livelihood Framework
SOZ	South Omo Zone
UNWTO	United National World Tourism Organization
VRM	Visual Research Methodology
WHO	World Health Organization

ABSTRACT

In recent times the tourism sector has been promoted as a major economic driver in Ethiopia for its major economic contribution to the national GDP, balance of payments, and employment, and as a source of foreign exchange earnings. Critics, however, have questioned whether this type of growth leads to wider socio-economic benefits and helps create a "good life." This research, a comparative case study, sought to determine the significance of cultural tourism in people's livelihood and its effect on the wellbeing of local people at tourist destinations. Two distinct ethnic groups in popular cultural tourism destinations in the South Omo Zone (SOZ), southwest Ethiopia, were selected as case study sites: A peri-urban village in South Ari Woreda and an agro-pastoralist village in Mursiland, Salamago Woreda.

The specific objectives were: (i) To illustrate the livelihood pattern of the local people in the two selected sites; (ii) identify assets that create opportunity in tourism as a livelihood resource; (iii) identify factors that drive local people to engage in tourism activities, and how they integrate these activities with their existing livelihood pattern to create the desired livelihood outcome; (iv) identify local indicators of wellbeing through participatory exercises and evaluate the benefits from tourism against their aspired wellbeing; and (v) assess local people's perception of their overall subjective wellbeing or quality of life (QOL), as well as tourism impact on economic, social, cultural and environmental factors.

A mixed-method qualitative and quantitative inquiry was employed in which in-depth interviews, focus group discussions, and a QOL survey were conducted to assess the perceptions of local people. 102 respondents, 51 in each research site, were engaged in both research sites in the QOL survey. In addition, a participatory visual research method (VRM) involved nine participants taking photos and videos as a way of learning visually from the local people's perspective. The fieldwork exercise was conducted during the wet and dry seasons and tourist seasons covering August–September in 2017; January–February and August–October in 2018; and February–March and August–September in 2019.

Chapter 1 details a literature review of the historical evolution of tourism in development and critics' concerns regarding the sector's role in addressing the wider socio-economic need of people since the 1950s. It also reviews the literature of tourism in the research sites, highlighting the lack of research xiv

devoted to understanding the significance of tourism in local people's livelihood and wellbeing, thus justifying a livelihood approach as the conceptual framework in order to examine the cases in a holistic manner. Chapter 2 details findings of local people in Kebelle A, South Ari, where they revealed cash from cultural tourism as critical to coping with vulnerable times arising from rain variability, pest infestations, and diminished public services such as water availability. Cash from tourism is mainly used to purchase food items and make ends meet, enabling women in particular to capitalize on their capabilities. A participatory focus group discussion of local people conversely revealed that the benefit from tourism was minimal compared to their aspired wellbeing, and their overall quality of life assessment on a Likert scale perception survey showed a moderate satisfaction level.

Chapter 3 reports the findings for the agro-pastoralist society in Mursiland, Salamago Woreda. The local people indicated that the income from cultural tourism is valuable for coping during vulnerable times like crop shortages due to recurrent rain variability, drought, and pest infestations. Cash from tourism allows them to avoid the sale of their valued livestock and empowers women. During a participatory focus group discussion, benefit from tourism was expressed as insufficient compared to their aspired wellbeing, but they evaluated their overall quality of life as satisfactory on a Likert-scale perception survey.

Chapter 4 reports the results of a participatory visual research outcome of local participants at two research sites that produced 940 photos and 10 pieces of video footage illustrating their livelihood, lived experience, and culture from their perspective. The exercise demonstrated their capability with digital visual expression and effective use of technology.

Chapter 5 details a comparative analysis of the two case studies based on selected livelihood approach variables such as assets, social relations, roles of organizations and institutions, and gender aspects of cultural tourism, as well as comparisons of two life stories, their evaluation of the benefits of tourism, and their perceptions of their QOL and the impact of tourism on the economic, social, cultural, and environmental aspects of their lives.

Chapter 6 concludes with a discussion of local peoples' perceptions of the significance of cultural tourism for their livelihood in the two case study areas. Local people in both case study areas conveyed that their vulnerable livelihood situation demands alternative livelihood strategies to cope and manage risk in the event of vulnerabilities due to internal stress and external shocks. In that, livelihood strategy in cultural tourism activities has created marginal benefit in the absence of other alternatives means. Women in particular gained access and control to cash income which otherwise was absent in the agropastoral communities. Local institutions such as guide associations which play a role in creating access to opportunities in tourism activities also act as gatekeepers limiting benefit from their engagement. The qualitative assessment of benefit and the Likert scale survey revealed the little gain observed is unevenly distributed among the local people in both research sites which calls for further study to distinguish who gains most and why.

CHAPTER 1

GENERAL INTRODUCTION

1.1　　Introduction

Tourism has become one of the major economic sectors in most developing countries because of its positive contribution to national GDP and employment and as a source of foreign exchange earnings, and due to its beneficial effects on the balance of payments, governments lately have focused on tourism development. Ethiopia has intensified its focus to make tourism one of its leading economic sectors, and as a result, new policy and strategy directions have been formulated to guide the sector's future development. Such focus on the benefits of tourism on the national and macro-economic level is dominant, while examinations of how the sector contributes to livelihoods at the local level is often muted. Examining tourism as an activity at the local level and considering its benefit to people at the local level started in the late 70s, with the study of alternative types of tourism that are small scale and engage the people, continuing with studies of tourism concerned with the green agenda and ecotourism in the 80s, and the pro-poor tourism in the new millennium; these have all contributed to the discussion of how tourism responds to people's livelihood at the local level. In a declaration, the World Tourism Organization highlighted that the success of the sector is ultimately to be measured by the increases in equality and the improvement of the quality of life of all people as its guiding principles in the early years of its establishment (WTO, 1980).

In cultural tourism, a global phenomenon that has no boundary, the primary interest is the local people, whose involvement is inevitably linked to their livelihood. Often, though, the extent to which their engagement contributes to their overall livelihood as well as their wellbeing, and even more so the degree of their agency in their engagement is often ignored.

This research aims to understand to what extent tourism, in particular cultural tourism, contributes to local people's livelihood and wellbeing from their perspective. Using ethnographic interviews, focus group discussions, and assessments of perceptions of the quality of life through a Likert-scale survey, the research demonstrates local people's perception of cultural tourism's significance on their livelihood and wellbeing.

This research through a livelihood approach, within a broader pollical ecology framework and a notion of actor-oriented analysis, builds on past research findings (1) to look at tourism within a wider perspective of local people's livelihood than just cash earning, (2) to give the local people the opportunity to express the significance of cultural tourism in their livelihood with first-hand evidence. Moreover, (3) it highlights the role of local people's cultural assets in creating opportunities to diversify their livelihood in times of vulnerability, demonstrating local peoples' sustainable resilience taking advantage of opportunities, in this case, cultural knowledge, and their identity as valuable means of creating alternative means of livelihood. (4) It further reveals how women gain access to cash income and control over cash, promoting their empowerment. (5) It has also applied a Likert-scale survey for the first time in the research areas to measure their perception of the quality of life associated with tourism, upon the assumption that their engagement in tourism may effect some changes in wellbeing, and to explore their view of the impact of tourism on four elements of life: the economic, social, cultural, and environmental. The exercise was undertaken with the involvement of local youth to understand the concept of quality of life, who interpreted it for respondents during the survey. (6) This research also highlighted new developments, in particular in the Mursiland tourist scenario, girls' agency in changing cultural norms in Mursiland irrespective of the external demand for an "exotic host culture," and the internal pressures for the pursuit of a livelihood.

This chapter has nine sections. This section comprises this introduction; the second section outlines the definition of tourism and cultural tourism; and the third section reviews the literature on the evolution of tourism and development studies and in the specific research area. The fourth section looks into the livelihood approach as the conceptual framework for this study, followed by the fifth section, which outlines the objectives, and the sixth, which presents the methodologies employed. In the seventh section, the research area will be introduced, and the eighth section explains the rationale for the selection of the research sites. The ninth section concludes by outlining the organization of the dissertation.

1.2   Definitions

1.2.1   *Tourism*

Tourism has been defined by academics, businesses, and governments from the perspectives of different disciplines. One early economic definition of tourism stated, "Tourism is defined as the science, art, and business of attracting and transporting visitors, accommodating them and graciously catering to their needs and wants" (McIntosh, 1977: ix, as cited in Leiper, 1979). In the anthropological field, numerous versions of definitions have been advanced; one is by Nash (1981:462), who defines tourism, putting the person in the center, as "the activity undertaken by a person at leisure who also travels." For Nash, tourism is defined by two elements of a person's circumstances, a need to travel and sufficient leisure time. Smith (1989:1) defines a tourist as a "temporarily leisured person who voluntarily visits a place for the purpose of experiencing a change." Tourism experiences have evolved over the years; likewise, it has become difficult to describe the experience in a particular way. Tourism has been transformed in the globalized world, where technology, communication, and transport have modified time and space, since the early traditional travel experiences, where very few individuals traveled to explore new parts of the world (Gomez, 2014). Smith (2014) elaborates Urry's (1999) "post-tourist" in the postmodern era as having evolved with the concept of tourism experience brought to one's home through television and the internet, contrary to past experiences.

To avoid confusion from the numerous attempts at a definition from different disciplines, the United Nations World Tourism Organization (UNWTO) uses a technical definition for governments and tourist organizations that monitor the size and characteristic of tourist market and businesses: "Tourism comprises the activities of persons traveling to and staying in places outside their usual environment for not more than consecutive years for leisure, business, and other purposes" (UNWTO, 2010). In this definition, there are three criteria: A tourist has to be out of his/her usual environment, no payment should be taken from the place where he/she is going, and the stay should not be more than a year.

One main point that we can identify in all of these definitions is a focus on just the tourist experience, without considering other elements within the tourism sector. Leiper (1979), a tourism specialist, is the only one to have attempted to illustrate the systems approach of tourism by detailing all relevant elements, each with distinct features that need to be considered in defining tourism. These broadly comprise the human element, the tourists; the geographical elements, which are the tourist generating region, the destination region or host locality, and the transit route; and the industrial element or tourist industry, which comprises tourism marketing, tourist carriers, tourist accommodation, tourist attractions, tourist services, and tourism regulation providers, indicating both governmental and non-governmental bodies (Leiper, 1979)

Nonetheless, even under this definition, consideration of the destination region does not elaborate on the different categories of people in the host country. Thus, in this section I would like to unpack this definition further and specify the different groups in order to identify the specific people, local people at the destination, that this research focuses upon. The category of destination comprises those places that provide services to tourism and also the local people who are the primary interest of the tourist in a cultural tourism setting.

1.2.2   *Cultural tourism*

Cultural tourism has also undergone an intensive process over the years of devising a working definition of the subject, mainly because it has been difficult to define the term culture itself, as it has both global and local significance (Smith, 2014), as well as due to the diversity of political and theoretical perspectives (Richards, 2015). Cultural tourism was initially identified as a niche market, but nowadays it covers a wide spectrum of tourism, with varied possibilities of tourism aspects such as architectural, art, heritage, religious, festivals, and indigenous sites, so much so as to suggest that all tourism might be termed as cultural (Smith, 2014). In order to avoid complicated discussions, I use here the latest technical definition of UNWTO (UNWTO, 2017:18, as cited in Richards, 2015:13): "Cultural tourism is a type of tourism activity in which the visitor's essential motivation is to learn, discover, experience and consume, the tangible and intangible cultural attractions/products in a tourism destination."

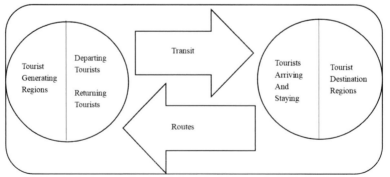

The Broader Environment: Physical, Cultural, Social, Economic, Political, technological

Figure 1.1: Tourism as a system

1.3   Literature review

1.3.1   Tourism and economic development

For years there has been debate on the extent to which tourism is an economic driver and what wider socioeconomic benefits it brings, particularly for local people at destinations. Looking at tourism beyond its economic advantages at the macro-level, this concern is particularly crucial in developing countries (Ali, 2016; Burns, 2008; Holden et al, 2011; Noveli, 2016; Telfer & Sharply, 2008) involving going beyond achieving economic growth to attain a "good life" that encompasses social, cultural, political, environmental, and economic aims and processes (Mihalic, 2014, Sharply & Telfer, 2015). The discussion goes far back, as many have tried to put the sector on a spectrum in terms of its wider contribution and effects beyond economic benefits to address the fact that GDP usually fails to capture the distribution of income across society and does not adequately measure the size of a nation's economy or reflect a nation's welfare (Stiglitz et al., 2009).

Early discussions in this line revolved around the argument that the economic benefits did not trickle down to the people (Harrison, 1992; Lea 1988; Smith 1989; Turner & Ash, 1975)   while it was promoted in the 1950s–1960s as a force to bring modernization and economic growth, with a trickle-down benefit to the poor (Telfer & Sharply, 2008). There was also concern over the effect of tourism on the culture that it priced and sold—the commoditization of culture—leading to the exploitation of the local host (Greenwood, 1979). From the point of view of political economy, tourism was also viewed more as a continuation of colonialism, a system of economic dependency of the local host (Hall & Tucker, 2004; Lea 1988). Alternative tourism initiatives involving the concept of sustainability and ecologically sound tourism as part of alternative development approaches were considered able to close this gap (Nash, 1996). In the new millennium, new initiatives for pro-poor tourism have attempted to implement tourism as forms of poverty alleviation programs (Ashley, 2000; Michael & Ashely, 2014). However, such initiatives have faced criticisms of their limitations in attaining their intended results in addressing equity and truly benefiting the poor beyond being "window dressing" or "tokenistic" (Scheyvens, 2007).

The World Tourism Organization (WTO) was initially set up as an organ of the United Nations in 1975 and later converted into a specialized agency of the United Nations (the UNWTO) in 2003. In the 1980s, the tourism debate was said to have been guided by a moral imperative (Scheyvens, 2007) emanating from a declaration prepared under the WTO, the Manila Declaration, which stated: "world tourism can only flourish if based on equality and if its ultimate aim is the improvement of the quality of life and creation of better living for all people" (WTO, 1980:1). In line with neoliberal ideology, viewing tourism as a poverty reduction mechanism, and following the UN Millennium Development Goals tradition, the UNWTO has committed to the latest UN Sustainable Development Goals (2015–2030) motto of "leaving no one behind," specifically committing to focus on Goals 8, Inclusive and sustainable economic growth; 12, Sustainable consumption and production; and 14: use of oceans and marine resources. The Sustainable Development Goals (SDGs), also known as the Global Goals, were adopted by all United Nations Member States in 2015 as a universal call to action to end poverty, protect the planet, and ensure that all people enjoy peace and prosperity by 2030 (UN, 2015).

It remains to be seen how these efforts will unfold at the national and local levels, particularly Goal 8, which includes the word "inclusive" in the original statement of the goal, "decent work and economic growth," as these goals are expected to be integrated within the government's national plans.

1.3.2   Literature review in the research area

Anthropologists since the early 70s have written on the relationship between the local people and tourists in South Omo Zone, and most have depicted tourism as an incursion into and a nuisance in local people's lives. Turton (1987, 1981, 2002, 2004, 2005), who conducted anthropological work in Mursiland, the homeland of an ethnic group and a major tourist attraction in South Omo Zone, has referred to local people's cash earnings from tourism in most of his works. In one work exclusively on tourism, Turton (2004) described the relationship between tourists and local people as a reciprocal act of feeding into each other: The tourist as an archetypal consumer but also the Mursi as an archetypal primitive, eager to be photographed to obtain cash (Turton, 2004). Abbink (2009) expresses the tourism experience of the Suri, another ethnic group in South Omo, as forming an uninterrupted continuity with the colonial past and colonial hegemony, an act that does not lead to better inter-cultural understanding and other such noble aims. Regi (2012, 2013, 2014), who also conducted anthropological work on tourism in Mursiland, focused more on tourism and its political dimensions, the tension between the local people and the state, and the role of tourism as a means of communication with the outside world for the local people, and also elaborated on how local people use different tactics to control tourist so as to earn cash, which he said has become the "new source of wealth" for the local people. LaTosky (2010) also reported on tourism as a source of new money for those who might not have access to material wealth, young girls and boys. Nishizaki (2019) also reported on cash income from tourism in Mursiland, as well as a new tourism initiative in Ari, creating a new source of earnings for the local people.

Table 1.1: Historical Overview of theoretical perspectives of tourism and development research

Historical evolution		
Liberal/neoliberal	Critical theories	Alternative development
1950s-1960s Tourism contributes to modernization through economic growth, employment, generation and the exchange of ideas. Benefits trickled down to the poor		
1970s on ward Foreign direct investment seen as the way to stimulate stagnating economies, investments in tourism adds a possible dimension attracting foreign exchange.	**1970s-1980s** Tourism associated with enclave development, dependency on foreign capitals and expertise; undermines local culture, social networks and traditional livelihoods	**Late 1970s onwards** Alternative form so tourism that are small-scale, involve education of tourism and more local control over tourism.
1980s on ward Tourism offers a way out of indebtedness "trade your way out of poverty"	**1980s on ward** Post-development view – 'local culture and knowledge' as the base for tourism. Tourism as solidarity and reciprocity.	**1980s on ward** The green agenda leading to the 1992 UN Summit of sustainable development. The introduction of Ecotourism.
Late 1990s onward Tourism as an economic sector that can contribute to poverty reduction. Public-private partnership encouraged.	Late 1990s onwards Anti-globalization lobby sees tourism as a way of advancing the force of capitalism into remote cultures. Post-colonial writers comment on the allure of the "other" – poverty attracts tourists; poor places as "authentic"; class difference between host and guest.	**Late 1990s on ward** Tourism offers poor communities a way of diversifying their livelihood options
2000s Under the UN Millennium Development Goals, tourism is made at the core of the economic development debate The Sustainable Development Goals (SDG). The 2030 development goals.	**2000s** Struggle in the determination of guidelines and parameters to establish tourism success in contributing to tourism. The failure of numerous ventures symptomize a failing global development agenda, which has at times been worsened by a 'poorism' mentality	**2000s** The main barriers to tourism and development emerge, which are linked to broader grievances about socio-economic development. Capacity building emerges as one of the key required actions to enable tourism to truly contribute to community development and empowerment.

Tourist cash for local people in the region was introduced gradually. In the early 70s, local people were initially shy and not open to new visitors in their territory, as key informants in the area recall. Then, since road access made it easier for mass tourists to reach the local people, the tourists introduced cash as a reward for the photographs.

As indicated earlier, although the cash earnings from tourism have been reported by most who have worked in the research area, there have not been studies of the contribution of tourism-related income to local people's livelihood, and in particular, the perspectives of the people themselves on its contribution to their overall livelihood are missing.

Thus, this research will follow a conceptual framework that examines life at a tourist destination, particularly the livelihood patterns of those whose lived experience, values, identities, and artifacts are the primary factors drawing tourist interest, in the hope that this will make it possible to understand how tourism activity is integrated within the wider local livelihood pattern and identify its contribution through observation as well as from local people's accounts.

Accordingly, this research has taken the livelihood approach as a framework with a notion of actor-oriented analysis to examine the significance of local people's engagement in the tourism sector as their livelihood strategy through the livelihood approach. The assumption is that looking closely and in detail into people's daily activity and their means of living and incorporating their own perspective on what benefits to wellbeing it entails might afford us insight into the extent to which the tourism sector, and in particular cultural tourism in this case, contributes to the local people's livelihood, and into its effects on their wellbeing.

1.4   The livelihood approach as a conceptual framework

The livelihood approach began in the 1980s following development anthropology, which dates back to the 1940s and marked a transformation in anthropology through the consideration of the social and cultural factors in development activities, the study of which originally focused only on economic factors (Lewis, 2005).

In such a situation, the livelihood approach emerged as a corrective measure. The approach was initiated by Robert Chambers in the 1980s and further developed by Chambers and Conway in the early 1990s. Later it was picked up by such scholars as Carney and Scoones in the late 1990s (De Haan, 2012).

The term "livelihood" has received many definitions, but that of Chambers and Conway (1992) has been prominence for years. The definition elaborated by Chambers and Conway (1992:) reads, "a livelihood comprises the capabilities, assets (including both material and social resources), and activities required for a means of living; a livelihood is sustainable which can cope with and recover from stress and shocks, maintain or enhance its capabilities and assets, and provide sustainable livelihood opportunities for the next generation; and which contributes net benefits to other livelihoods at the local and global levels and in the short and long term."

In this definition, the element of capability is associated with Amartya Sen's definition of capability (Sen, 1984:198 as cited in Chambers & Conway, 1992:4), referring "to being able to perform certain basic functioning's, to what a person is capable of doing and being, these including being adequately nourished, to be comfortably clothed and to avoid escapable morbidity and preventable mortality, to lead without shame, to be able to visit and entertain one's friends, to keep track of what is going on and what others are talking about." Chambers & Conway, 1992: 4). This is associated with a quality of life in which one has valued activities and the ability to choose and perform those activities. Chambers and Conway (1992) also state that capability has diverse meanings to different people and in different places, including the criteria of the wellbeing of people. In addition to Sen's definition, Chambers and Conway (1992) expand the definition of capability, suggesting another subset of characteristics, including being able to cope with stress and shocks and being able to find and make use of opportunities within one's livelihoods.

Furthermore, in their definition Chambers and Conway (1992) highlighted that equity implies the equal distribution of assets, capabilities, and opportunities, and an end to deprivation and discrimination among those who are weak and marginal. In terms of sustainability, the connotation is refined beyond the everyday use of sustainability, which is mostly associated with environmental sustainability, referring for example to pollution, limits to growth, global warming, and physical degradation. Not departing too far from this view, sustainability in Chambers and Conway (1992) specifically is brought down to the local level and related to people's livelihoods, in which case it refers to self-sufficiency, self-restraint, and self-reliance, thus referring to the ability to maintain and improve livelihoods while maintaining or enhancing the local and global assets and capabilities on which livelihoods depend (Chambers & Conway, 1992).

The livelihood approach seeks the core elements of livelihoods, making it ideal for examining local people's lives at the micro-level and for studying the lives of people in a more structured way. De Haan (2012) points out, for example, that (1) its approach places people at the center of study, studying their livelihood strategies in terms of resources or sets of assets or capital; (2) it places greater emphasis on people's opportunities to exercise agency rather than on their impoverishment or the focus of the survival studies of the 1980s; (3) it affords us the opportunity to look beyond just the lives of the people to also examine the structures governed by institutions, for, as de Haan explains, "rainfall is bounded by climate, the land is placed in the property systems, and wages and prices are ruled by supply and demand in markets and government regulations," and thus by looking wider in this way, it allows us to give consideration to the structures that either enable or prevent people from organizing effective livelihood strategies; and (4) it also points out, at times, the potential of people's agency to influence these structures.

Critics have charged that the livelihood approach ignores the discourse of power relations, but De Haan (2012) also elaborates how that element has been addressed by works such as Blaikie et al (1994) in the area of human and political ecology, Rowland (1997) in gender studies, and Long (1992) on political arenas.

It is also said that the livelihood approach has lately examined how to make linkages between the local into the global (De Haan, 2012). In the study of tourism, a global phenomenon, the livelihood approach then becomes the ideal choice for analysis at the local level.

1.5   Objectives

The overall objective of this study is to understand local people's perspectives on the significance of cultural tourism in their livelihood and its effect on their wellbeing. The specific objectives are:

1. To examine the livelihood pattern of local people in two cultural tourism destinations.
2. To identify assets that create new opportunities for tourism as a livelihood.
3. To identify circumstances that drive local people to engage in tourism activities.
4. To develop local indicators for wellbeing through participatory exercises, and for valuing the benefits from tourism against their indicators (Chambers, 2008.112).
5. To assess local people's perception of their overall subjective wellbeing or quality of life (QOL).

1.6   Methodology

This research followed a comparative case study methodology and used a mixed methods approach of both qualitative and quantitative methods, with more focus on the qualitative methods. For secondary data, a literature and policy document review was conducted. Primary data were collected through ethnographic field research using in-depth interviews for two life stories, 30 key informant interviews in Jinka to gather general information on the tourism context within the zone, and unstructured interviews with 10 people (9 women and 1 man) in the peri-urban setting in Ari, comprising the total number of people engaged in the tourism initiative in the research site. In Mursiland, interviews were conducted with 39 people (8 men, 31 women) and six focus-group discussions were held (four all women, one all men, and two mixed groups), and in addition observations were made of 95 women and girls. Occasional conversations with tourists during tourist encounter at research sites were conducted to gather reflections on their experiences.

In a Likert-scale survey of their perceptions of subjective wellbeing or life satisfaction, 51 respondents were selected at each of the research case study sites using a purposive sampling method. In addition to my participatory-observation, a visual research methodology (VRM) was incorporated within this research, under which nine research participants were involved in gathering photos and video clips from both research sites, selecting their own sites and themes to produce the footage.

In order to ensure the validity of results, triangulation through verification of facts was performed through discussion with relevant key informants at both sites. All qualitative data were analyzed thematically. The fieldwork was undertaken during the dry and wet seasons: August–September in 2017, January–February and August–October in 2018, and February–March and August–September in 2019.

As a way of ensuring informed consent, all research participants were provided with a thorough briefing on the nature of the research at all times.

1.6.1   Sustainable livelihood framework checklist

A sustainable livelihood framework (Scoones, 2009) that corresponds to the livelihood approach was used as a checklist in order to illustrate the tourism activity within the mix of the local people's livelihood strategies and elicit its significance from participants' perspective. The framework elaborates on five main categories of capital that correspond to assets in the livelihood definition: natural, physical, human, financial, and social capital as an input.

In the description of assets, a sixth category of capital, cultural capital, is added to the framework. This type of cultural capital aligns with the definition of Throsby (2012), which describes it as both an intangible and a tangible cultural capital. Here the focus is on intangible capital that is directly associated with the knowledge systems, ideas, practices, beliefs, traditions, skills, and experiences of people that serve to identify and bind together a given group of people, which he distinguishes from other types of cultural capital such as the cultural capital of Habitas posited by Bourdieu (1986), among others (see Table 1.2).

Intensification as a livelihood strategy is related to expanding or increasing an already existing strategy, for example, in agriculture or pastoralism, such as adding more land for the production of crops or grazing, or changes in technique to improve production (Ellis, 2000).

Diversification is a livelihood strategy defined as the process whereby rural households construct an increasingly diverse portfolio of activities and assets in order to survive and to improve their standard of living (Ellis, 2000). According to Ellis (2000), diversification is determined by two elements, choice and necessity. Necessity is due to distressful reasons, while choice refers to a voluntary and proactive reaction. In most cases, coping strategies determine diversification as a strategy to cope with stressful situations when households face vulnerability in their livelihood. Vulnerability is a high degree of exposure to risk, shocks, and stress, as defined by Davies (1996). Risk strategies are proactive actions for the future to avoid anticipated risk (Davies, 1996); seasonality is another determinant of diversification.

Migration is a type of livelihood strategy where one or more family members leave the resident household for varying periods of time to contribute to the welfare of the household (Ellis, 2000). It can also be taken as one type of diversification mechanism in peoples' livelihood strategy.

Scoones' (2009) provides a wider perspective on the livelihood framework beyond just the microeconomic view of livelihoods, highlighting the need to paying special attention to issues such as knowledge, politics, scale and dynamics. In this research, therefore, within the broader framework of political ecology, it has attempted to look into politics in terms of power within and beyond the local structures affecting local livelihoods, the scale of potential local and international trends that exert local effects, and dynamics in terms of people's initiatives, local knowledge as resources for resilience.

The framework therefore utilized as a tool to visualize how the tourism activity in the two selected research sites fits within local people's livelihood strategy and the extent to which it affects their wellbeing, considering the wider perspective of their livelihood. The framework provides a structure within which to locate local people's livelihood pattern, and the approach inherently facilitates capturing local people's perspective at the micro-level (Agrawal et al., 2014; Manosa, 2019; Scoones, 2009) considering the social, political, cultural, and environmental aspects. This parallels Burns' (1999) suggestion that tourism is better studied from a holistic view of development as a system that makes up part of a wider social and cultural system than through an isolated economic study. In this regard, this research will also seek to examine local people's livelihood as impacted by tourism at a micro level from a holistic perspective.

A participatory asset mapping methodology (Dorfman, 1998; Lightfoot, Mccleary & Lum, 2014) was also used during the FGD to assist local people in identifying the resource base that enables them to build their existing livelihood in a participatory manner.

Table 1.2: capital/assets, adopted from Scoones (2009)

Categories	Description
Natural capital –	Natural resource stocks (soil, water, air, genetic resources etc.) and environmental services (hydrological cycle, pollution sinks etc.) from which resource flows and services useful for livelihoods are derived.
Economic or financial capital:	Infrastructure, the capital base (cash, credit/debit, savings etc.), infrastructure, and other economic assets which are essential for the pursuit of any livelihood strategy.
Human capital	Skills, knowledge, ability to work and good health important for the successful pursuit of livelihood strategies.
Social capital	Social resources (networks, social relations, associations etc) upon which people draw when pursuing different strategies.
Physical capital	Buildings, irrigation canals, roads, tools, machinery, even a house as a means of earning an income through rent or used as a business as a source of livelihood.
Cultural Capital	Knowledge systems, ideas, practices, beliefs, traditions, skills and experiences of people comprising sets of ideas, practices, beliefs, traditions and values of people

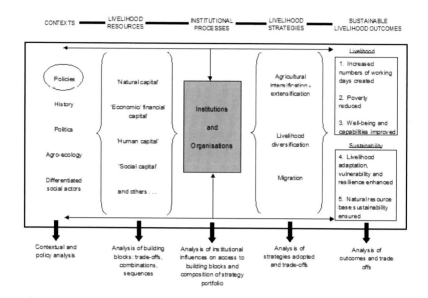

CONTEXTS —— LIVELIHOOD RESOURCES —— INSTITUTIONAL PROCESSES —— LIVELIHOOD STRATEGIES —— SUSTAINABLE LIVELIHOOD OUTCOMES

Figure 1.2: Sustainable livelihood framework

1.6.2   Wellbeing assessment

Wellbeing does not have a straightforward definition as yet, but researchers often use wellbeing and quality of life (QOL) interchangeably (Dodge, Daly, Huyton, & Sanders, 2012; Uysal et al, 2015) therefore, here we will use the World Health Organization's definition of (QOL) as "an individual's perception of their position in life in the context of the culture and value systems in which they live and in relation to their goals, expectations, standards, and concerns." (WHOQOL, 1998:551).

Moreover, as a way of more closely examining the effect of tourism on local people's wellbeing, two ways of assessing wellbeing were used: A participatory wellbeing indicator identification exercise using a focus group discussion (Ochieng et al., 2017), and a Likert-scale subjective wellbeing assessment measuring the perception of quality of life or life satisfaction. For this, a Likert rating scale of five choices ranging from *highly satisfied* to *highly dissatisfied* was used.

Subjective wellbeing was scored on a Likert scale. Although my research is predominantly qualitative, incorporating a quantitative method was expected to enhance the explanatory method (Camfield et al., 2008), as in recent years, subjective wellbeing or QOL measure research has gained new interest in evaluating tourism benefits from the host people's perspective (Uysal et al., 2015). As a result, a Likert scale response is assigned numerical values and the mean values computed. The main purpose is to identify the general tendency of the local people's perceptions of their subjective wellbeing or life satisfaction (Sullivan & Artino, 2013). In the case of subjective wellbeing, one is measuring psychological constructs such as life satisfaction, perceived QOL, happiness, or life fulfilment as opposed to objective wellbeing, given by traditional economic measures of social development, for example, gross domestic product (GDP) (Sirgy, 2002, Uysal et al., 2015). This is because once tourism is introduced in an area, it is thought that the quality of life or wellbeing of people is expected to be affected either positively or negatively (Uysal et al., 2012, Woo et al., 2012).

The Likert scale has five scores for responses: *highly dissatisfied* (1), *not satisfied* (2), *moderate* (3), *satisfied* (4) and *highly satisfied*, in response to 13 questions regarding four categories of life satisfaction domains (Annexes I & II). The domains were based on Cummins' (1996, 1997) factors of life satisfaction: material, community, emotional, and health and safety wellbeing. These categories also align with Chambers' (1992) capability definitions and wellbeing, which Scoones (1998) reiterates, as discussed above. For this exercise, 51 people in each research site were interviewed ages between 16 and 81, with disaggregation of male and female participants: in Kebelle A (female 21, male 30) and in Mursi (female 27, male 24) (Table 1.3). In addition to the QOL survey, a questionnaire was administered on the perception of the impact of tourism along four dimensions: economic, social, cultural, and environmental. The Likert scale for impact perception has five scores: *strongly disagree* (1), *disagree* (2), *not sure* (3), *agree* (4), and *strongly agree* (5).

1.7   Research area

1.7.1   *Tourism in Ethiopia*
Ethiopia has intensified its focus on tourism as one of its leading economic sectors, and as a result, new policy and strategy directions have been formulated to guide the future development of the sector. With the first tourism office established in 1962 under the imperial regime, the sector has passed through different phases of focus in line with the respective government's policy direction. After the end of the imperial era in 1974, the sector stagnated for almost three decades with restrictions of free movement of tourists under the socialist

government, the Derg, due to civil war and drought (World Bank, 2006). The sector again started to register gradual growth since 2001 under the government's partially managed neoliberal market economy, allowing the travel and tourism sector to operate freely, unlike under the previous government, under whose socialist ideology tourism was strictly closed off. As a result, the tourism sector reported registering a contribution to the country's GDP at 0.77% in 2008 (Ali, 2016). The total GDP contribution is forecasted to rise by 4.9% (9% of GDP) by 2024. In 2013 (UNECA, 2015).

Table 1.3: Likert scale survey respondents' age and sex data

Categories	Description
Natural capital –	Natural resource stocks (soil, water, air, genetic resources etc.) and environmental services (hydrological cycle, pollution sinks etc.) from which resource flows and services useful for livelihoods are derived.
Economic or financial capital:	Infrastructure, the capital base (cash, credit/debit, savings etc.), infrastructure, and other economic assets which are essential for the pursuit of any livelihood strategy.
Human capital	Skills, knowledge, ability to work and good health important for the successful pursuit of livelihood strategies.
Social capital	Social resources (networks, social relations, associations etc) upon which people draw when pursuing different strategies.
Physical capital	Buildings, irrigation canals, roads, tools, machinery, even a house as a means of earning an income through rent or used as a business as a source of livelihood.
Cultural Capital	Knowledge systems, ideas, practices, beliefs, traditions, skills and experiences of people comprising sets of ideas, practices, beliefs, traditions and values of people

Today, the Ministry of Culture and Tourism (MCT) of Ethiopia combines two sectors, Culture and Tourism. The first tourism development policy was enacted in 2010, alongside a five-year plan (2010–2015) as part of the first national Growth and Transformation Plan (GTP I). In 2015 the country's second five-year plan of the Growth and Transformation Program (GTP II; 2015–2020) revising GTP I by upgrading the tourism sector from a cross-cutting sector to one of its seven main economic sectors alongside agriculture, manufacturing, mining, construction, urban development and housing, and trade (Federal Democratic Republic of Ethiopia, 2016). The primary aim of the new direction was intended to contribute to the overall sustainable socio-economic development of the country by creating a coordinated and integrated system and enhancing community participation.

Today, the Ministry of Culture and Tourism (MCT) of Ethiopia combines two sectors, Culture and Tourism. The first tourism development policy was enacted in 2010, alongside a five-year plan (2010–2015) as part of the first national Growth and Transformation Plan (GTP I). In 2015 the country's second five-year plan of the Growth and Transformation Program (GTP II; 2015–2020) revised GTP I by upgrading the tourism sector from a cross-cutting sector to one of its seven main economic sectors alongside agriculture, manufacturing, mining, construction, urban development and housing, and trade (Federal Democratic Republic of Ethiopia, 2016). The primary aim of the new direction was intended to contribute to the overall sustainable socio-economic development of the country by creating a coordinated and integrated system and enhancing community participation.

In 2015, through an initiative driven and supported by the Intergovernmental Authority on Development in Eastern Africa (IGAD) to drive the socio-economic development of the regional economies, Ethiopia produced the sector master plan, the Ethiopian Sustainable Tourism Master Plan (ESTMP) for the years 2015–2025. The main aim of the ESTMP is to establish a national framework for sustainable tourism development, with the aim of contributing to socio-economic development and poverty alleviation. The high growth target aims at 5 million international visitors in 2025, with corresponding increases in receipts from international arrivals from a baseline of ETB 14.197 billion in 2012 to 180 billion in 2025; and with the number of jobs rising from 985,500 in 2012 to 4.8 million in 2025. The ESTMP, therefore, sets out 10 strategic pillars, priority projects, and activities in a long-term implementation framework covering 2015–2025 (UNECA, 2015).

1.7.1.1   *Policy review*

All the latest statements of national policy directions, starting from GTP I, GTP II, and the Sustainable Tourism Master Plan, have highlighted the aspiration for sustainable tourism development. The sustainable tourism master plan, which reflects these policies, classifies its strategies under 10 thematic areas or pillars: 1) Policy, regulation and institutional framework, 2) Tourism product development, 3) Tourism marketing, branding, and promotion, 4) Investment in tourism facilities and series, 5) Human resource development, 6) Tourism support infrastructure and services, 7) Tourist safety and security, 8) Tourism research and development, 9) Conservation and preservation of national and cultural resources, and 10) Tourism development finance. A total budget of ETB1602 million is earmarked for the 10-year implementation period. These strategies and actions are founded upon a number of fundamental principles, among which are the issue of sustainability, to ensure economic sustainability for all stakeholders and contribute to poverty alleviation, environmental health, and respect for the social-cultural authenticity of the host community; stakeholder engagement; and high-level tourist satisfaction.

As its main guiding principles, the master plan states the principles of inter-generational and intra-generational equity, which are the main equity principles in the sustainable development declaration (UN, 1992). It also puts community participation and empowerment as its value, ensuring host communities` full participation in the country`s tourism development and making them beneficiaries of skills training, funding and market access, as well as including them in the policy formulation spaces to ensure their integration in to the tourism industry value chain (UNECA, 2015:103–104).

These institutional moves and policy commitments, as well as strategic directions, indicate the country's vision for the sector in terms of accommodating the diverse stakeholders within the tourism sector. However, it is important to look beyond the policy provisions to understand the extent to which the implementation of these policies can have a meaningful impact on local people's lives, in particular, local people at tourism destinations.

1.7.2   The South Omo Zone (SOZ)

This research purposefully selected two tourist destination sites as case study units in SOZ in the Lower Omo Valley, Southwest Ethiopia. The ESTMP identified two existing major tourism resource products in the country, the Northern Historical Route, where the historical heritage is the main focus, and the Southern Route of Culture and Nature. SOZ, within the Southern Nations, Nationalities Peoples Region (SNNPR), is the main destination within the Southern Route of Culture and nature. The tourism scenario in SOZ is characterized at the national level as the "Ethiopia's Cultural Mosaic of Ethnographic Attractions," for it hosts 16 ethnic groups with distinct cultures, languages, and traditions for the attraction of local and international visitors at all times.

The total population size of the zone is 573,435, with an average population density of 31.7 persons per sq. km (CSA, 2008a, 2008b). The zone is divided into eight woredas (equivalent to districts), five of which comprise agro-pastoralists. Six of the eight woredas are cultural tourism destinations, five of which are in the

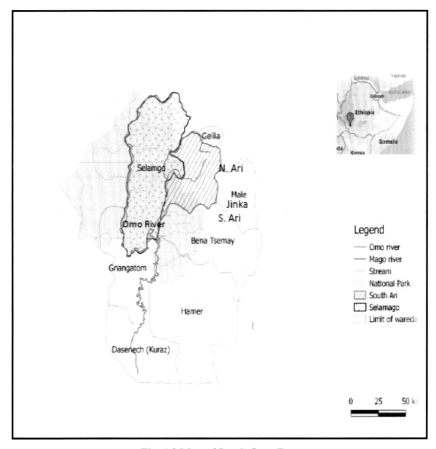

Fig. 1.3 Map of South Omo Zone

lowland agro-pastoralist areas (Figure 1.3). The lowest altitude in the Zone, about 376 meters above sea level, is located at the extreme southern point of the zone, near Lake Rudolf; and the highest peak, Shengama Mountain, about 3,418 meters above sea level, is located in South Ari Woreda, the northeastern part of the zone.

Informants in the Zone indicate that the main tourist attraction from early on has been and still is the people of the zone and their cultures. In the early days, since the opening of the Mago National Park in 1972, tourists came mainly to visit the people. The Mursi and Hamer were said to generate the most popular tourist interest among the ethnic groups in the zone. The Mursi villages were far apart, so tourists had to stay overnight to visit different villages. At the time, wild animals could be sighted, but the cultural events—markets in Key Afer and

Walduba on Tuesdays, Dimeka on Thursdays, and Turmi on Sundays—were the main interest. The park also was an attraction on a second stage.

Major tourist attraction sites in the zone are the Mago National Park, Omo River, Wollishet, Sala Controlled Hunting Area, Buska Natural Forest in Karo, Fejej, Kibish, and Weyto Bola Archeological and Anthropological Sites, South Omo Research Centre and Museum, Lakulan, Maki and Tuket Hot Springs in Salamago, Gicha and Bombi Caves in North Ari, murile ostrich breeding in Humer, the Salamago, Chelbi, and Tama Wildlife Reserves in Salamago Woreda, and cultural attractions of pastoralist markets.

The Zone reported 42,524 tourism visitors in 2015, of whom 55.8% were foreign tourists and 44% were categorized as domestic tourists. Domestic tourists include people coming for short-term work stays in the Zone following opportunities in the newly established sugar factories by the Omo River. The zone also reported earnings from tourism reaching a total of ETB 30 million in the year 2015 (Zonal Office data, 2018).

Unfortunately, under international human rights sanctions due to corporate social responsibility for violations of the rights of indigenous people as a result of investment activities in areas where the land title is contested and involuntary resettlement is occurring, the tourist destinations are under a ban until all violations have been investigated and remedied (EU, 2018). Nonetheless, 30% of Ethiopia's tourism market is from Europe, and tourists from the UK, Germany, Italy, and France are in the top ten sources of visitors even today (Netherlands Ministry of Foreign Affairs, 2018).

1.8   Rationale for the selection of the research case study areas

Prior to the selection of the two sites, I had the opportunity to travel around SOZ to identify my research site. The two sites, Kebelle A in Jinka, a peri-urban village in South Ari, and Mursiland in Salamago Woreda, were the final choices. I consulted with an informant to ensure my plans were realistic. To research two sites and with a tight schedule, proximity and ease of access were my criteria, but also the need for two different settings to examine diverse elements and maximize the findings. Thus, Mursiland, 70 km away from Jinka, and Kebelle A, about 3 km away on the periphery of Jinka, seemed ideal places to begin my research. The combination was perfect in terms of the diversity it offered for study. I feel that it requires a lifelong engagement that not just one study can fulfill.

I have always wanted to understand the tourism scenario in South Omo because I was puzzled by the number of pictures and video clips one can find on the internet, particularly tourist attraction points in the agro-pastoralist areas. It is my wish to learn about their life and the reasons that they have opened their life to tourism when their life seems to be much more secluded from the world. This is because the pictures also depict a unique culture not only to the international world but also for those of us coming from the highlands in the north. It was an opportunity to go closer and to learn, and an even better chance for research.

Deep within, I did wonder how much tourism impacted the people. Are they aware? Is it their choice to be engaged in such a way? From the beginning, I had promised myself to be open and only seek to understand from their perspective; knowing what I know, I said this should be their say. I will take what is there as I see it and also what they say it is.

1.9   Organization of the dissertation

The dissertation is organized into six interrelated chapters, including the concluding chapter. Chapter 1 will present the introduction, literature review on tourism in general and specific to the area of this research area, the conceptual framework of the research, objectives of the research, and detailed methodology employed. Chapters 2 and 3 will present the findings of the two case studies, a local initiative in a peri-urban village within the Zonal city of Jinka in Chapter 2 and an agro-pastoral village in Mursiland, Salamago Woreda, demonstrating cultural tourism scenarios of "Photos for Cash" in Chapter 3. Chapter 4 will discuss an exercise of the participants in a visual research methodology (VRM) as part of the participatory observation of the research, the results of the exercise, and reflections on the exercise. Chapter 5 will present a comparative assessment of the two case studies through selected variables from the livelihood approach and results of the valuation result of tourism benefit, perception of QOL as scored on the Likert scale, and the impact of tourism on the four elements of economic, social, cultural and environmental aspects. Chapter 6 will provide a detailed summary of the previous chapters, three discussion points, and the overall conclusion of the research.

1.9.1   Research limitations

The sample size constitutes a limitation on the overall results for both case sites: In Ari, the number of households involved in the tourism sector is limited, while in Mursiland circumstances of accessibility and security hindered research somewhat. Still, all possible measures have been taken to maximize data gathering. For example, in Ari, when administering the Likert-scale questionnaire, other villages within similar initiatives were included to increase the number of respondents. In Mursi, respondents visiting tourist sites during tourist encounters in research sites were used conveniently to maximize the diversity of voices.

CHAPTER2

THE CULTURAL TOURISM SCENARIO IN KEBELLE A, SOUTH ARI

2.1 Introduction

This chapter will introduce the cultural tourism scenario in a peri-urban area of Kebelle, South Ari, referred to in this document as Kebelle A. Cultural tourism in Kebelle A is an initiative by young local guides exclusively working in South Ari based in Jinka Town. The initiative also operates in three other Kebelles within the city of Jinka. Thus, Kebelle A is the subject of one case study within the comparative case study of this research.

Jinka Town is a hub for the tourist influx on its way to the main tourist destinations. South Ari people have not been a focus of tourism as such until very recently. The Ari territory, however, is one area anticipated to be developed by the local tourism office as an eco-tourism spot. This chapter will try to examine the new initiative of cultural tourism that has engaged the local people of the Ari ethnic group since 2012 and its significance for their livelihood.

This chapter will demonstrate the overall status of livelihoods in Kebelle A and the significance of cultural tourism as a livelihood strategy from the perspective of the local people at the destination as a contribution toward understanding their coping and risk management during vulnerable times, particularly as to how women, as the majority engaged in the initiative, gained access to cash and capitalized on their cultural assets and capabilities. However, the value benefit from tourism is minimal, and they indicated their quality of life/life satisfaction as moderate. Local people in Kebelle A perceive tourism as having no negative impact on the social, cultural, or environmental elements in their area. This chapter will also look into their identified wellbeing indicators and the value they place on the benefit from tourism based on their aspired wellbeing, their perception of their overall quality of life/life, and their perception of the impact of tourism on economic, social, cultural, and environmental issues.

2.1.1 Background

The Ari people speak Araf, *Ari-af* (Gebre, 2015); during the late nineteenth century, Emperor Menelik's expansion southward brought Amharic-speaking migrants, whom the Ari called the *Gama,* into contact with the Ari people.

The Ari people inhabit the southern highland and western side of the Rift Valley, near the highest peak, Mt. Garagir (3,375m above sea level), with diverse vegetation ranging from lowland Acacia savannah (500–800 m) to Afro-Alpine vegetation (Shigeta, 1990). The Ari people, inhabiting the two woredas of the South Ari and North Ari area, are the most populous within the zone, with a population of 283,125, making up 48% of the total population of the Zone. The territory is divided into a highland, *dizi,* and a lowland dewlap, and its climate is characterized by the dry season, *hassin,* and wet season, *bergi,* as a result of which the Ari cultivate diverse crops categorized into two groups, according to Shigeta (1990). The *ishin,* category, consists of grain crops such as barley, sorghum, tef, maize and pulse crops such as lentil, pea, and faba bean, while the second category, *tika,* includes yam, taro, *enset,* coffee, and other vegetable crops.

Early accounts prior to 1941 reveal that the Ari had chiefdoms headed by ritual kings called *baabi* (Naty, 2002). The chiefdoms (known at the time as Baaka, Kuree, Shangama, Beya, Siida, Woba, Barged, Gayl, Argen, and Gooza) were engaged in wars among themselves until the Imperial army of Haile Selassie defeated all the chiefs and conquered the territories, instituting a new feudal system of serfdom called *ye-gebar-sirat* in 1941, under which Ari families were assigned to imperial soldier-settlers, not only paying an annual tribute of cash and in-kind, but also performing labor services with their families for the soldier-settlers (Naty, 2002). The Ari, now divided into North and South Ari, were part of the then Gamo-Gofa Province set up during imperial times. The Ari depended on the cultivation of *enset,* sorghum, maize, and vegetables, and raising sheep in the highlands and cattle in the lowlands (Naty, 2002).

Between 1974 and the early 1990s, the socialist Derg regime made radical changes in the structure of the Ari people's life, enabling them to repossess their land through a land reform policy ending the feudal system. Not long after, a villagization scheme in Aariland was introduced, which brought down families from the mountainous areas to Bakko, Alga, Arkisha, Gedir, Kaysa, Kuree, Sheepi, and Zomba in a forced settlement. At the time, the scheme was intended to bring households closer to the gridline and also provide basic services such as health, education, and clean water (Naty, 2002). This was known as the rapid rural transformation, allowing greater control of the peasant farmers (Tadesse, 2002). This, however, was not appreciated by the people.

During one reporter's fieldwork, an account of a metalsmith who was moved with his family to Kaysa at that time recalls that:

> *People were moved to those villages because the land was steep and not recommended for farming.*
>
> *Some of the families, however, moved further down to settlements near Jinka or returned to their original place, for they did not find the new place conducive to their life. Jinka was established with people coming from surrounding villages, such as Dimeka, Key Afer, Kako, and Kaysa. (Interview, 2019)*

Another metalsmith, M.A., among the local people who have moved from Kaysa, recollects:

> *...most of the people who moved down were artisans, people who are potters and metalsmiths. They were identified as the caste of the 'manna,' considered as the lower caste within the Ari population. Until the time the socialist government took over, these people were looked down upon by the Ari people. As a result, eredy did not inter-marry or enter the homes of ordinary Ari families. The situation has changed since the Derg regime to some extent. Still, the sentiment can be found. (Interview, 2018).*

Similar categories of people are located in neighboring ethnic groups such as Gofa, Basketo, Maale, Oyda Gamo, and Walaita, according to Freeman and Pankhurst (2001) and Kaneko (2005).

Just after the Derg regime collapsed and before the Ethiopian People's Revolutionary Front (EPRDF) consolidated power in the region the situation was in turmoil during the power vacuum in the local administration. MK recalls violent raids between ethnic groups to the west of the Omo River in villages in Bench Maji, which was then part of the Gamu Gofa Kifle Hager. The raids were led by the neighboring ethnic groups from the Surma and Mursi to take their cattle.

Once the new government of the EPRDF fully controlled stability some families crossed the Omo and Mago National Parks and moved into Ari territory for safety.

My host recalled her life right before the change of government and the emergence of the EPRDF.

...we arrived in Ari fleeing the turmoil in Maji, west of the Omo River. My
father who owned numerous cattle was under attack and was killed by the
Mursi people who took all our cattle in raids during the change of the
government. My mother was pregnant and gave birth to a baby girl who she
named.

2.1.2   *Jinka*

Jinka is the Zonal Administration town within the territory of South Ari. Jinka
is also a hub for tourists coming to the Zone. A senior local authority, D.G.,
recalled Jinka Town in the 70s: "the center for Jinka city was at *Shola sefer.*
Tourists used a local *Buna Bet* (a kind of pension) called W/ro Nigatwa
Abbeb—Albergo—near the current market. There were no tourist and destination
arrangements there at the time, even until the late 80s. The area was under the
administration of *Gamgofa Teklai, Gizat Yegelebna, Hamer Bako Woreda. At* the
time no standard hotels were available to receive the tourists that started to arrive.
The then Administrator, Ato Teferra Endalew, advised some investors in town to
take land and build hotels. As a result, hotels such as the Orit, Goh, and Omo
Hotels were built through such a scheme, and provided tourists more space for
bedding, food and resting place."

In the early 60s, the Tourism office was under the Amhara region Cult
ure, Tourism and Communications - amara *killel, bahil, tourism ena- masta-
wekiya* (BATUMA), then changed to be named Culture, Communications an
d Tourism - *bahil, mastaweki ena* tourism (BAMATU) ; then it was transfe-
rred to the Trade, Industry, and Communication Bureau - *nigd,* industry *en-
a* mastawekia biro, then again changed to Culture and Tourism *bahil ena* tou
-rism. Now, it is under the Culture, Tourism, and Government Communicat
-ion Affairs - *bahil,* tourism *ena, mengist mastawekia gudai.* This serves to
show the repeated change of affiliation of the office, which, according to
the informant, was a major problem in its stability as an institution, and fo
cuses on its mandate to manage tourism issues in the Zone. Since this inte
rview in 2018, the affiliation has already changed to Culture, Tourism, and
Sports Department.

In the 70s, there was no good road connecting Jinka to Addis Ababa. The only
road that came through Welita took one week to reach Jinka because of the bad
road condition. Tourists coming to visit the area had to stay up to a month and
could only access most of the villages with hard-top land cruisers. A tarmac road
was not constructed until 2012/13. The National Tourist Organization (NTO)

opened an office in Jinka in 1991 and introduced a small airplane, a Dash 6, which started to bring tourists to Jinka, sometimes up to four times a day. The small airplane, carrying about 17 people back and forth from Addis Ababa, was the only convenient transportation for tourists. After a few years in service, that was also discontinued for about ten years and only resumed in 2018 (interview with key informants in 2018).

2.2   Kebelle A

Kebelle A (the smallest administrative structure) is located 3 kilometers away from Jinka. This Kebelle has 3149 inhabitants (2732 male and 1426 female) and 430 households (351 male-headed and 79 female-headed households; local Kebelle information, 2018). It was a rural village, one of the Kebelles within South Ari Woreda until it was included within the territory of the city of Jinka in 2015 as a peri-urban village. The Kebelle is still a farming community. Kebelle A is about 37.8km away from the Mago National Park from its northeastern side.

Still an agrarian community, 95% of the population are still farmers, with 5% engaged in other city-based employment. However, according to the local administration, this trend is rapidly changing due to land fragmentation with an expanding population. As a result, inhabitants need to engage in alternative livelihood options.

2.2.1   The livelihood situation in Kebelle A

2.2.1.1   Land ownership

Kebelle A, now an urban administration, faces difficulties administrating a system that is still rural within an urban setting. According to the Kebelle administrator (2018), agriculture is still, by and large, an important means of making a living. Thus, the main challenges are associated with the land. The size of land plots in the village is getting smaller due to population pressures; as a result, the sizes of farmers' landholdings are shrinking. Table 2.1 shows the size of landholdings of households in Kebelle A, where those that own 4 hectares (16 timad) of land or over make up 25%; 1 hectare, 25%; and 0.5ha or less, 50% of those that own land. Households in the second category have shared their land with their children. Those in the third category are those engaged in other city-based activities, for example, running small businesses or working in the city as guards or day laborers in combination with farming.

In Kebelle A, the main produce comprises maize, sorghum, teff, millet, and kidney beans. Enset was the main staple, but today its use is reduced, particularly in this part of Ari. The local officer believes that this reflects the local people having lost their skills and knowledge of preparing the crop for food consumption.

2.2.1.2   Women's land ownership

Land ownership by women in Kebelle A, as in all of the Zone, is recorded with her as a co-owner with her husband. This means the ownership certificate will include the wife. If the husband has a second wife, as it is customary but not officially recognized, it will be up to the husband and the family to make arrangements to divide the common land among his wives. The second or third wives do not have any legal recognition, but it is customarily understood that the land is agreed to be a common resource.

Table 2.1: Farmland ownership in Kebelle A

8 *'Timad'*: 1 ha

	Category	Land size Hectare/Timad	% of population
1	Sufficient	2ha. (16 Timad)	25%
2	Medium	1 ha. (8 Timad)	25% [1]
3	Small	0.25ha.(2 Timad)	50% [2]

2.2.1.3   Youth employment and agricultural activities

Youth unemployment is a major problem, yet those who have the opportunity to own land are losing interest in continuing in the agricultural sector. There are 245 youth farmers, of whom 74 are registered as female and 171 male youth farmers.

Young people, after finishing school, are no more interested to engage in agricultural activities, dominantly subsistent crop production. Lately, the local agricultural administration is promoting urban agriculture offering training and credit facilities for youth to diversify their self-employment options. Areas of opportunities range from livestock fattening and intensive farming in small farmland for vegetable production to poultry.

2.2.1.4   Soil and water conservation activity

Steep land prone to flooding is common in the area. Thus, the local authority mobilizes inhabitants for training and physical labor 30 days per year to conduct soil and water conservation, and stone and soil bund work in degraded areas. This also serves to maintain and improve flood management, *Gorf-maswetch sira* (Amharic word). Extension officers from the Kebelle agricultural office also provide training on utilization of fertilizer (NPS: nitrogen, phosphorus, and sulfur) and improved seeds to sell to local farmers to improve productivity.

2.2.1.5   Health status

The village shares a health post with six other Kebelles. The Kebelle health office provides basic services such as vaccines and training for mothers on pregnancy and nutrition.

Malaria is a major problem in the area. As a result, DDT is sprayed in the homes once in a while. However, inhabitants told me they try to avoid the spray by pretending they are not at home, because they have experienced respiratory illness due to the spraying. Still, this practice continues during major malaria seasons right after the rainy season. Alternatively, mosquito nets are provided to homes for protection from mosquito bites.

According to Kebelle health officials, water-related and water-borne diseases, parasites, and bilharzia are some of the recurrent health problems in the area. There are inadequate toilets, and road access to remote places hinders ambulances from reaching mothers during labor.

A new national social protection scheme has operated since 2018, and local people are enrolled if they are able to pay an amount of 305 ETB ($10.79) per year per family. This allows them to receive coverage for all health services, including medicine. Local people are enrolling, but already the service is receiving criticism as medicines are insufficiently available.

Those that can prove that they are the poorest of the poor are given free access to the scheme through an identification card attesting their status.

2.2.1.6   Access to water

Water shortage is a major challenge in the area. Three potable water points erected in the area are often out of order, local people used to depend on natural springs, which are now drying up, and the perennial River Neri, whose water is used for all purposes such as cooking, washing clothes, bathing, car washing, and more.

A local monastery in the area provides 20 liters of water every day for each household from its water point. As the pressure is huge, the water point in the Monastery is often also out of order; therefore, households often lack basic drinking water for days. Recently, the Agricultural Research Institute located in the village has been making an effort to solve the water problem partly by supplying the village with groundwater.

2.2.1.7   *Report of recurrent rainfall variability*

Persistent rainfall variability has had serious impacts on the Kebelle farming systems. In 2016, the failure of the *belg*, or short rainy season in March and April, which precedes the long rain, or *kremt*, in June, July, and August, led to increased stress as the *belg* and *meher* harvest failed. As a result, food rations were distributed in the area to compensate for the failure (Kebelle Agricultural Head interview, 2017). Furthermore, the erratic rain patterns have led to the failure of inputs such as fertilizer and improved seed, which normally are bought by farmers, putting inhabitants in an impoverished state where they lose their investment as well as the anticipated produce from their investment. Figures 2.1 and 2.2 present the rain and temperature data for 2007–2017, showing the monthly average trend of temperature and rain variability, as well as the variability of the *belg* rain.

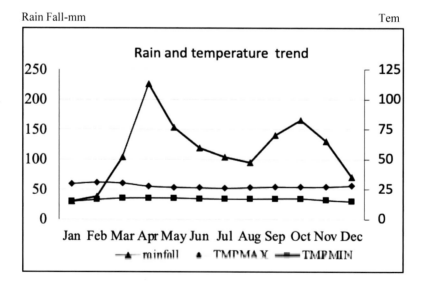

Figure 2.1: Rain and temperature data, 2007–2008

Rain Fall-mm

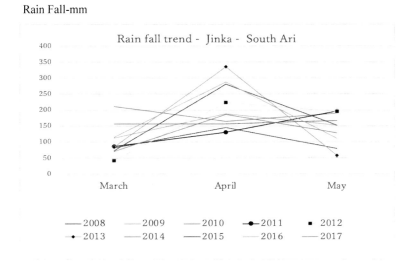

Figure 2.1: Belg rain variability, April–May

Pest infestations are due to the variability in rainfall, as in the recent incident of an armyworm infestation within the region following an overwhelming rainfall, which led to a loss of harvest in 2016–2017. This pest crisis has been reported elsewhere in Africa and in regions of Ethiopia such as Amhara, Tigray, Gambela, Oromia, and SNNP since 2016 (Assef & Ayalew, 2019).

2.3   Cultural tourism scenarios in Kebelle A

Selected households in Kebelle A receive calls from the local guides operating in South Ari, based in Jinka, asking if they will be ready to receive a tourist or tourists for a visit. Local artisans engaged in local crafts are the main targets that the guide association has established to be the focus of tourist visits. In Kebelle A, households engaged in *areke,* a local grain-based liquor making; *injera* making (the staple Ethiopian flat bread, made of teff); a household holding the Ethiopian coffee ceremony; and a potter and a metalsmith in the area are visited by the tourist in one trip. These people are normally engaged in these activities as their main means of living, with the exception of the person organizing the Ethiopian coffee ceremony. The households who participate in the visit can change depending on who is ready for the visit.

...the guide brings the tourists to visit us. The tourists come to see what we do. We are happy to show them our work, this is what we do to make life, we are happy if they like to come and see our work. (A young women making areke in Kebelle A)

2.3.1   A local initiative

The initiative was started by the local guide group in the town of Jinka, representing the South Ari ethnic group. Based in a place called Gardab, Jinka City, the guide association was established by the merger of two guide associations in 2016 as *Akimi, Yenegew Sew*, meaning "Tomorrow's future for humanity." At the time, the zonal administration banned more than one guide association within tourist-visited woredas; therefore, the two guide associations had to merge and form one association.

The members of the guide association took the opportunity to expand their guide services for tourists visiting an ethnic group adjacent to South Ari, Mursiland, and a major tourist attraction in the Zone. Early in the morning, the tourists visited Mursiland but did not have activities in the afternoon upon their return. In this stretch of time, the guide decided to organize tourists to visit Ari villages in the vicinity of Jinka. Four Kebelles in Jinka were targeted, of which the site for this case study is one. The artisans were settled in those villages during the villagization scheme during the Derg regime in the 1970s. In each village, the number participating in the tourism activity is not great. In this particular research site, the regular participants comprise about 11 households, with some occasional increases in number.

The initiative can be described as a "local-people-led" tourism, but quite distinct from schemes such as community-based tourism or ecotourism. The terms community-based tourism or eco-tourism initiatives were defined as those that are attached to conservation and development projects with the objective of contributing to the conservation of natural resources as well as benefit the community living near protected areas (Dodds et al., 2016) or those that are based on the development of community-owned and managed lodges or homestays (Goodwin & Santilli, 2009). These types of initiatives are often managed with support from external bodies such as non-governmental organizations with limited participation from the local community. In such initiatives, local community capacity and knowledge to run such schemes were described as limited or even nonexistent, therefore requiring crucial support from external bodies (Moscardo, 2008).

This local initiative, however, is quite distinct in that the scheme was initiated by the local guides themselves without any outside involvement. They identified an opportunity to start a unique program for tourists as an extra activity and, in turn, provide extra income for the local people at the destination to strengthen their livelihood. In this way, it can be said that the assumption that local people lack the skills and knowledge to start or organize such community-based schemes can evidently be dismissed.

The villages targeted for the scheme are indeed in close proximity to one of the protected areas in the Zone, Mago National Park, except that there is no conservation program linked to the tourist visits active at the moment. However, tourists come to the area mainly to visit the Mursi ethnic group who inhabit the forested area near the protected area.

2.3.2   A day in the tourist destination village—South Ari

Households that are involved in the tourism activity in Kebelle A mainly make their living by engaging in their daily activities, and the visits from tourists are an additional benefit, an opportunity to supplement their livelihood. Therefore, it is highly anticipated. However, there is no exceptional preparation to be done to receive tourists. Their day's work has its own sequence of tasks, so their priority is to complete the day's planned sequence, during which they might receive a call from one of the guides alerting those interested in showcasing their work that a tourist group will be visiting, as they may be out of their workplace to fetch water or firewood to the mill or market. In this situation, if one is not able to show her/his work, the next household will take the chance. It is always chancy, but the visits from tourists normally take place at a usual time, so they organize their daily activity away from their workplace at times when tourists will not normally be visiting. For example, they will go to fetch water early in the morning, to the mill late in the afternoon, and to fetch firewood at mid-day.

This is because tourists coming to visit Kebelle A come mostly in the afternoon, after their early morning visit to Mursiland and after their lunch. Sometimes, after tourists arrive in Jinka, their first visit may be an Ari village, with their other trips planned for the next morning. In this case, a trip to Ari villages may take place late in the morning or still in the afternoon.

In addition to the crafts and work of the local people, the tourist also gets the chance to glimpse the typical Ari lifestyle, their huts and traditions, and the market within the city of Jinka Town. This arrangement has become quite popular, so that all travel agencies from Addis Ababa make an advance booking for all groups that visit Mursiland in order to expand their tourist experience in the area.

2.3.3   Local people's reflections on tourists

The visit of tourists in the village is perceived by many as more than just coming to visit their work. In some instances, there have been tourists who developed an instant liking of some children in the village, so they want to support their education by helping their families with monthly stipends or family support. At other times, some tourists come with clothing, sweets, pens and pencils, and exercise books to give to children. As a result, when tourists come to the village, if it is not during school days, all children follow the tourists in the hope that they will have something special for them. Most tourists like to interact with the children; therefore, they are followed by an entourage of children.

In this case, the local people await tourists in the anticipation that some of them are there not only to visit them for their pleasure but have come with different missions, mostly to provide some kind of support in their life's difficulties. This is not unfounded, for while the cases may not be many, in the case study village, a potter with five children is receiving regular yearly support of cash and clothing from a family abroad. The occasional provision of a large amount of money just because a tourist liked a certain mother or child is a story often told again and again, increasing the anticipation of the local people, for the hope of someone granting them such a surprise is always in their minds. I thus asked them what tourists are in their view. One informant, a metalsmith, expresses his feelings about tourists visiting thus:

> ...tourists do not just come to visit as tourists; I think they are looking for new ideas. They are looking for innovative ideas. I have myself experienced this, a tourist wanted to try what I am working on, and he was so happy to try that he rewarded me with 100 ETB ($4). I don't feel they come with any bad intention; I feel it is for good.

2.3.4   A love-hate relationship

The tourist exclusively visits households engaged in craft activities, rather than just tourists wandering around the village to look at people's living style. The scenario is different in the zone, were tourism focuses on random photography of the people through direct transactions with cash. The tourist visit is focused on the activity and the crafts, not the people as such. The initiative is unique, a genuinely local idea creating new interests for tourists to expand their experience. This has created a lucrative business for the guide association that generates a regular income for the members, as well as for their association to continue as a solid organization supporting its members.

The association, as explained in 2017 by the chair of the association, charges each tourist 700 ETB ($18), which then is divided into: 300 ETB ($11) for the attending guide, 100 ETB ($4) deposit for the association, and a tax (8%), 20 ETB ($0.72) to be put aside as contribution toward young students in the city who are not able to afford their teaching materials at the beginning of each year. This particular act has earned this guide association special regard from the zonal office as a socially responsible group giving back to its community.

The rest of the money will be divided among the local households who showcase their craft, food, and beverage-making businesses. Normally, households will receive up to 150 ETB ($5) for 20 tourists in a group; 100 ETB ($4) for 17 tourists, 60 ETB ($2) for 10 tourists, and 35 ETB ($1) for 1–9 tourists. These rates are arbitrarily set by the association, where members of households have no discussion or agreement as participants in the scheme. The relationship between the members of the association and of the households is thus a love-hate relationship, for the households believe that the visit of the tourists is dependent on the guides' goodwill. One tourist group will always visit households making metalwork, pottery, *injera*, and *areke*. Households ready on the day will participate once they agree to show their work. Photo 2.1 shows a tourist encounter in Mursiland.

Photo 2.1: Tourist encounter

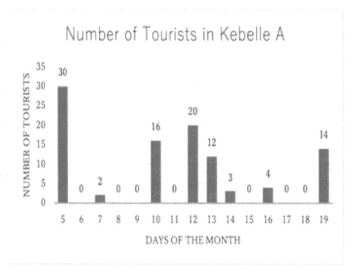

Figure 2.3: Two-week observed tourist visit data

Those involved in the scheme anticipate receiving tourist visits throughout the day, as a result of which they earn some cash.

However, upon discussion, they find that what they earn is far from what the chairman of the guide explained to them. They often complain that after visits, it is difficult to collect what they earned in a timely fashion. They often have to chase the guides to remind them of amounts owing and demand their payment of past visits while they are engaged with tourists visiting. Figure 2.3 shows a two-week tourist flow record in Kebelle A. During that period, local people did not receive the full earnings indicated by the guide association.

In this two-week period, local people could have received at least 100ETB on days 5 and 12, but on those days local people complained that the guide did not hand over the cash due. Normally they will receive money, but not on the day of the visit, and the amount will not be exact. A.M., from one the participating households complains,

> A lot of tourists are visiting, but we do not get equivalent cash for the number of visits. We have to wait for the guides to give it to us later, but it is hard to get the money sometimes. Still, we are happy they bring the tourists to us.

2.3.5   *Stakeholders*

In this initiative a number of stakeholders participate between the tourists and the local people they encounter. The stakeholders are at the national, zonal, and woreda levels, and each has a role in accomplishing the tourism scenario. As a result, the tourism scenario engages a number of stakeholders who also benefit from the activity, both directly and indirectly. Here we discuss the main stakeholders within the scenario. The full structure is illustrated in Figure 2.4.

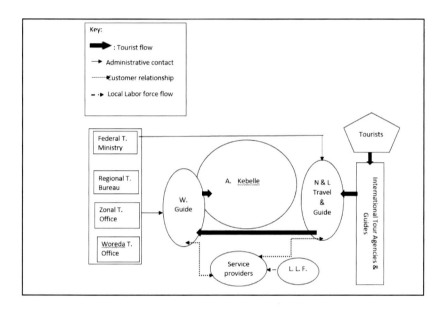

Figure 2.4: Schematic of the tourism scenario stakeholders

2.3.5.1   *The local people*

Local people are those who participate in the new initiative in Kebelle A and are the primary interest of the tourist. They are directly involved in the tourism activity, showcasing their culture, lived experience, and knowledge. In this case their existing livelihood activity is embedded in the local culture; their engagement is not recognized by the local authority that regulates the tourism activity. Therefore, their activity is informal and not visible in the tourism structure. This has led to complaints of their working relationship with the guide association that initiated the scheme of tourist payment standards, thereby leaving them vulnerable in being powerless to correct the transaction.

2.3.5.2   The local guide association

The local guides are the initiators of the scheme in South Ari. Their main activity is to link the tourists with the local people who showcase their artisanal work in four villages in Jinka Town. The connections with local households in the four villages are solely their own contacts, and other guide groups could not work with the households without their knowledge. Recently some youths within Kebelle A have requested links with the initiative; however, the rule of only one group of guide within one woreda has solved the conflict, leaving the scheme the sole responsibility of the guide association that initiated it. However, the local authority has insisted that they incorporate some youths within their association. This has created another conflict between natives (from the local ethnic group, Ari) and non-local youths, which is the basis for the right to work in the area. This is now the latest problematic conflict in Ethiopia, where people are discriminated against in a place where they lived for generations for not being from the recognized ethnic group in the area. This has thus created a problem in Kebelle A as well, as some youths were not able to join because they are not from the Ari ethnic group, which has created another conflict within the village and between youths. In all these conflicts, the youth guides have started to abandon Kebelle A to avoid this conflict.

2.3.5.3   National level tour agencies, and guides working for tour agencies

These are normally based in Addis Ababa and form contacts with the local guide association, in this case either contacting the zonal guide association to make arrangements with the woreda guide group or directly making arrangements with the woreda guide association. The national level travel agencies are not allowed to visit local sites without the knowledge and accompaniment of the local guides so as to prevent the loss of benefits to the local guide.

2.3.5.4   Zonal local authorities

The zonal local authorities are responsible in regulating the tourism activity within the zone. This includes all the guide associations at the zonal and woreda levels. They also have the responsibility of regulating service providers such as hotels, lodges, and restaurants, as well as monitoring the flow of tourist into the zone and woredas. As a result, they demand regular reports from the guides and service providers, particularly hotels and lodges, on the activities and flow of tourists. Once in a while they organize trainings for the guide association to improve their guide services. The zonal authorities, however, do not have any direct contact with the local group in Kebelle A but receive indirect information from the guide associations. This can be taken as evidence of neglect of the local authorities of their responsibility to provide support and assistance to those engaged in the sector.

2.4   Livelihood assets of local people engaged in tourism

Households engaged in tourism activities in Kebelle A pursue diverse livelihood activities along with the artisanal work that is the main attraction of the tourist. In order to distinguish the main assets that local people depend on to establish their livelihood, nine household members (three men and six women) participated in a one-day focus group discussion exercise to undertake asset mapping (Lightfoot et al., 2014). During the FGD, participants identified their main asset base, *habte*, that enables them to access their livelihood in general. Assets or capital within the SLF is defined by Ellis (2000:31) thus: "… stocks of capital that can be utilized directly or indirectly to generate the means of survival of the household or to sustain its material wellbeing at differing levels above survival." The assets identified are categorized according to the asset/capital in the sustainable livelihood framework. More information gathered from observation and during interview has also been added to the identified asset list through focus group discussion exercises. Figure 2.3 shows a transect map prepared by members of Kebelle A to identify assets within their village according to their listing during the focus group discussion.

2.4.1   *Natural capital*

2.4.1.1   *Forest*

The forest near the village, *Olgen*, is an area providing access to land for cultivation; grazing for cattle; and forest products such as fuel wood, charcoal, honey, and medicinal plants. Recently, part of the land has been acquired by the new university in the Zone, Jinka University. As a result, local people feel that some of their source of livelihood has diminished. The rest of the forest is also owned by other governmental institutions, such as the local prison; as a result, women in particular complain that their access to resources of fuel wood in the forests for home cooking and also for their businesses has been denied. They say that free access to the forest has been a major advantage for most of them, who are unable to buy firewood for cooking, and also for those engaged in small businesses. The proximity to their village was also advantageous, but now they have to go far out into the forest to collect wood, which requires extra effort by women. Photo 2.3 shows firewood collection in the nearby forest, *Olgen,* which normally takes an hour round trip, and another hour to collect wood.

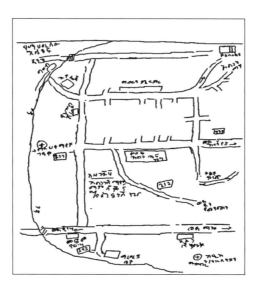

Figure 2.5: Transect map of Kebelle A.

Photo 2.2: Asset mapping by participants in Kebelle A.

Photo 2.3: Firewood collection

2.4.1.2   Land

The main cultivars in the area are crops such as maize and *teff*, grown in the steeper land. They cultivate crops twice a year, maize in the first *belg* rain beginning in March, and *teff* in the second main *kiremt* rain starting in July. Produce is for subsistence with some occasions for market to raise cash. For the most part, *teff* is a lucrative cash crop, but maize is only sold to raise cash for certain household needs, according to those who cultivate.

Cultivation of *enset* (false bananas) is not habitual here, unlike most parts of Ari, particularly in the North Ari area, where it is a main staple. According to the local people, the crop is said to have been infested with an unknown plant disease, so it has not been possible to propagate the plant. As a result, it is not a main staple today in this part of Ari. I observed that some heads of the plant still remain in the home gardens of some homes, where the leaves are used for wrapping during baking. These home gardens provide coffee, fruit such as mangos, avocados, and medicinal plants.

2.4.1.3   *Water*

Access to water, *lokki*, is mostly from the perennial River Neri; pond water, *tolli lokki*; and the springs *tuti lokki* and *koita lokki* near the village, which provide their daily needs. However, these spring waters are drying up, causing concern to all the local people.

Three potable water points in the vicinity have been erected, but all three are out of order; therefore, all use natural water bodies as sources for all their household and business needs. Collection of water from the river and springs involves a distance on average of a walk of some 20 minutes each way carrying a 20-liter jerry can, which, if not coming from the monastery, is not drinkable. This puts a huge strain on women due to the distance and the quality of water. According to Ethiopia's Universal Access Plan (UAP) the minimum standard for rural areas is defined as at least 15 liters of safe water per person per day within 1.5km of their home (Butterworth et al., 2013).

In 2019, the agricultural research institute in the local area attempted to respond to the dire need of the local people by digging wells for ground water to provide potable water. Local people have said that this has created some relief after years of difficulty.

Communal pit-latrines are available for households to share; for example, my host family shares one dry pit latrine with four other households, 13 persons in total; and there is one public latrine in the vicinity of the village.

2.4.2.   *Financial capital*

Their livestock, cattle and small ruminants, are a source of cash for households. Farmers also sell their produce in the nearest market. Small businesses such as pottery making, metalsmithing, *areke* and *borde* (a grain-based local beer), spices, and *injera* are other financial sources.

2.4.2.1   *Iqub*

A local scheme called *iqub* is an important means to raise cash in many villages and towns in Ethiopia, constituting a social banking system, defined as rotating savings and credit associations (Kedir & Ibrahim, 2012). The total amount that is rotating in the village is ETB 50,000 (USD 1,804), but this amount is divided among a number of interested people enrolled in the scheme. One person's share is normally ETB1000 ($36); however, the majority of people in the village are not able to raise this amount of money, and as a result they share the single share among 10 or 20 people. The draw comes out every week, and the winners share the amount received according to their contribution.

2.4.2.2   *Saving and credit scheme*

Furthermore, recently the women have been enrolled in a credit and saving scheme whereby every week they save ETB ($0.07) and hold a social weekly gathering where discussions of essential issues such as marriage, inheritance, and gender issues are held. The initiative was created by an NGO operating in the area as a women empowerment scheme to encourage saving and credit as well as discussions among the women every week. They say that it has helped them immensely, because "we discuss things we normally do not talk about. Even our marriage problems with our friends."

In addition, the local micro-finance scheme, a government initiative, provides a saving and credit scheme for the local community. Farmers enroll to gain access to credit and saving, and female-headed households operating small businesses will also join the scheme. This type of individual saving and credit is preferred by most to the group-based saving and credit scheme which requires collective collateral limiting independence of individual flexibility. Although the group-based scheme avails a better credit facility in terms of financial accessibility.

2.4.2.3   *Iddir*

A local *iddir*, a form of an indigenous social insurance whose main function is to help members during bereavement (Pankhurst & Haile Mariam, 2000), is also available. The scheme is a system where members contribute a certain amount of money every month. Thus, the *iddir* will provide an amount decided by the association to help the family during bereavement to cover necessary expenses and social requirements. In the village members pay 10 ETB per month, and during a bereavement the family will receive 600 ETB ($27.65). However, not all are members of the *iddir*, as it is difficult to raise the monthly payment.

2.4.2.4   *Cash from tourism*

Tourism cash is reported as one means to access cash in Kebelle A. Those engaged in the tourism activity appreciate the extra cash that they receive, however meager. They said it is something they cannot ignore as it covers some essential needs on the day. If it were not for the guide's difficult behavior, they feel that they could have gained much more, considering the flow of tourist into their village. Photo 2.4 depicts a metalsmith at work who is participating in the tourism initiative.

Photo 2.4: Metalsmith at work

2.4.3   *Physical capital*

Local people in Alga identify the markets, *gebeya*, in their vicinity as essential for their livelihood. Two market options are available in the area: Jinka on Saturday and Arkisha on Tuesday. These markets offer the opportunity to exchange produce such as chicken, goats, milk, the grain *fatir*; *enset akime*; the fruits *akka-aff*; African Moringa *kalangi*, aleko, gomen; metalwork products such as knives and ploughs; pottery; *areke* (grain-based liquor); fuel wood; *injera*; and grass for cattle fodder.

In addition, local churches, schools and the one road with a bridge over the river Neri is identified as the physical assets. Recently, construction of a second bridge is underway, which will provide an alternative route to the center of town. are connected to the central town and the Arkisha market in Jinka.

People also utilize their homes as a place of production and a place to sell their produce. Those engaged in food and beverages in particular take advantage of this. Others who own their homes rent rooms to increase their monthly income.

Limitation of water supply hinders local people in their livelihood activities, especially those engaged in the food and drink business. Access to electricity, as households lack their own access point and are forced to share, is also a major issue that is raised as a problem.

Alternatively, mobile phones have improved local people's effective communication in their business activities. This is especially important for their engagement in the tourism activity so as to communicate with the guides.

2.4.4   Human capital

The majority of the local people are farmers who depend on cultivating their land. There are also those that have skills and artisanal knowledge, which provides a basis for their livelihood. The local households depending on their crafts, artisanal skills, and local knowledge of crafts make a living thereby, at times as their sole source of livelihood. Single mothers involved in making pottery, *areke*, or *injera* lead lives based on this capability. It can also supplement their main livelihood, where the husband is a farmer and the wife has skills in pottery or other capabilities to supplement their livelihood.

A health facility is provided by the Kebelle; the recently started social protection is also available but still all people are not enrolled in the scheme. There are three school, all elementary, two teaching grades 1–4 and one 1–8. All students beyond grade nine have to go to the adjacent Kebelle or to town in Jinka.

2.4.5   Social capital

Their social network is identified as an important asset for local groups to access opportunity in building their livelihood.

Social contacts and acquaintances, "knowing people" or *ed kikn esmeti*, is a key factor for a person to do well in life, as expressed by the group. That is, in everyday life their livelihood is dependent on how well they engage with their community. In the case of engagement in the tourism activity, households with good relationships with the guide association receive continuous visits from tourists, which result in cash earnings. Likewise, all advances in life are explained to have been secured through the quality of contacts and acquaintances.

The local people in Kebelle A have strong extended family ties in the neighborhood. The majority of people are in extended families living close to each other. Furthermore, social groups are formed based on religious affiliation among the Orthodox, Muslim, and Protestant communities, which have their own social support mechanisms by affiliation.

2.5   Assets and livelihood strategy drivers in cultural tourism in Kebelle A

Local people's access to tourist visit in Kebelle A is usually modified by two factors: First, their cultural asset, the traditional capabilities or knowledge they acquire, and second, their social capital in their social relations and networks. Local people also indicate vulnerability in their livelihood as a driver to seek diversification of cash in cultural tourism.

2.5.1   Cultural assets creating opportunities for livelihood

Local people's cultural asset, skills, knowledge system, and experiences, which already provide a means of living for the local people, have recently received special attention from tourists. The opportunity is therefore determined by the capabilities of the local people in such artisanship. The majority engaged in such activities are women, including pottery making, *injera* making, *areke* making, metal work, and preparing coffee. These activities normally enable women to start a living easily with minimal input, depending on the skills and knowledge they acquired from their families. These skills and knowledge systems have now created opportunities for them to engage in the tourism initiative. As a result, more women are engaging in such activities, especially *areke* making and *injera* making, in order to share the opportunities for tourist visits, thereby enabling them to diversify their livelihood and obtain extra cash to boost their income. According to Ellis (2000:15), diversification is defined as "a process by which rural households construct an increasingly diverse portfolio of activities and assets in order to survive and to improve their standard of living."

Occasionally, though not frequently, some people who are not involved in tourism activities do gain the attention of some tourist and receive cash. This often resembles winning a lottery prize. Photo 2.5 shows a potter displaying her work.

2.5.2   Social assets determining livelihood opportunities

Local people's cultural assets on their own do not ensure their engagement in the tourism sector. Local people's good networking ability determines their access to the opportunity of being visited by tourist. As observed and also reported by informants, there are some people who have the skill and knowledge but are not involved in the initiative. Therefore, all those with good relationships with guide

Photo 2.5: Potter's work

association members receive visits and thereby income from tourist visits.This means that their access and opportunities are determined by their social relations, as it has been noted elsewhere (Haan & Zoomers, 2005).

A lot of tourists come here, but the money we get is not as agreed, 100ETB is very rare and a lot of groups with more than ten come often to visit. I sell my products and they give me 100ETB for any product, while I normally sell, for example, a big pot for 30ETB, a coffee pot for 10ETB, or a flat injera maker for 50ETB in the local market. However, the guides do not allow this unless we share the money we earn. I have 4 children, I am a widow, and I have a twin, I sell firewood to get more cash ...one lady felt sorry for me and started sending me 1000ETB ($37) every year until now. She comes and visit us. She said she is turetegna–a pensioner, but she said she wanted to help.(A.M, a potter, 2018)

Mobile phones also play a huge role in this regard, and being connected at all times ensures the opportunity. Thus, all of them keep their mobile phones close for updates from the guides on a daily basis.

2.5.3   Vulnerabilities as drivers for livelihood strategies

Local people in Kebelle A report that vulnerabilities associated with internal stress as well as external shocks cause them a daily struggle to make ends meet.

2.5.3.1   Rain variability and pests

Local people were complaining in 2017 of poor harvests. E.K. reported, "normally maize will be sold as *eshet* just before it is harvested; now that this is no more available, grain was destroyed by pest after a heavy rain." Informants also said that farmers used to sell their produce to the village people before taking it to the market, but in 2017 they were not selling any grain as their harvest was not good.

> *We have not seen a year like this with such incident with pests. An invisible thing consumes the maize and turns to it into porridge.*
> *I did not want to put out pesticide, as it killed cattle that came in contact with it. I said I will do without it, now I have to do it myself by hand, I have lost half of my harvest, but I am ok with it. (Informal conservation with a female farmer, August 2017)*

In 2017 everyone in the village was talking about the pests in their field. There was also the problem that farmers were trying to remove the worm physically, and the contact was giving them sore fingers and they had to go to the health center. This was also reported by Kebelle agricultural development agents during my interview in 2017. This involved the fall armyworm (FAW; *Spodoptera frugiperda*), which is still a problem in other parts of Africa as well as in Ethiopia, in the regions of Amhara, Tigray, Gambelia, Oromia, and SNNPs (Fanta & Dereje, 2019).

2.5.3.2   Grain price fluctuations

The local people engaged in the tourist initiative in village A depend on the market to purchase grain for their consumption and their business. In particular, those producing food and beverages for business purchase grain from the market. They then face the challenge that the market price for grain fluctuates due to drought and pest infestations in the Zone. This puts stress on their food consumption as well as their business input. In the years 2017, 2018, and 2019, the variability in rainfall and pest infestation have affected the grain price, in turn affecting the households in their consumption needs and their businesses. This was also reported for those years during my interview at the Kebelle office.

2.5.3.3   *Fuel wood scarcity*

In normal circumstances, local people collect all their fuel wood from the nearby forest. However, the amount of forest cover is diminishing, so people cannot access fuel wood in closer proximity, and farm encroachments into the forested area and institutions taking land for construction have all reduced the size of the forest. This forces the local people to purchase fuel wood from the market, which due to the resulting scarcity leads to price increases too great for the local people to absorb. This is even more so for those engaged in small businesses.

M.K., engaged in *areke* making, explains her need for fuel wood for distillation: "The forest land is changing into farm land fast, so we have to go far to collect wood, as we are not able to purchase wood from the market. Until recently one bundle of wood used to sell for 40 to 50 ETB ($1.44–1.80), but now the price of fuel wood is increasing, and has reached 70ETB ($2.52). As I need a lot of wood to make my *areke*, the only option is to go far to collect wood."

The fuel wood challenge also is compounded due to fuel wood usage, which is highly inefficient, as local people still use open fires without any techniques to save energy. It seems that such techniques have not been introduced at all in the village, so people still use firewood in an open *'sost gulicha'* style, a traditional system using three stones to support their cooking pot as a stove for cooking. This open fire is said to waste energy (Photo 2.6).

Photo 2.6: Open fire cooking

2.5.3.4.   *Water shortages*

Water shortages make it hard for most small businesses to continue operating. As potable water is not available, they have to collect water from a nearby spring or river. As businesses need more water, they have to purchase it. For one jerry can of water at the potable water source, it is only necessary to pay 1 ETB ($0.036), but if they have to buy it, they will pay 5 ETB ($0.18) to private homes with tap water, which increases their expenses. Operating with marginal business capital, households face difficulties with price increases from such expenses.

2.5.3.5   *Government response*

In times of major vulnerability due to external shocks in the area, the local authority provides support and assistance, in particular to farming communities. This was evidenced in the 2016 and 2017 rain shortage and pest infestation occurrence, where the government provided food aid in the Kebelle.

2.5.4   *Local people's responses in times of vulnerability*

2.5.4.1   *Coping strategies*

Local people in Kebelle A increasingly depend on the available natural resource base in the case of internal stress, where basic services fail. Their only means to survive in this regard is to depend on natural resources to ease the need for cash. Fuel wood and water are predominantly utilized from the nearby forest, river, and springs even when the distance is a challenge and the encroaching urbanization rate is increasing.

2.5.4.2   *Modifying business inputs*

Another means is reducing their business scale. In times of stress, the inputs to their business are reduced to match the amount they can afford. This affects their income and overall livelihood, especially for those whose livelihood depends solely on their small businesses.

2.5.4.3   *Modifying the number and type of food consumption*

Local people report that modifying type and quantity of food consumed as a means of coping in time of food shortage due to times of vulnerability. Most people responded to the question of how many times they eat per day, saying only twice. They also adjust the type of food consumed. Taro *godlore*, *posessi* (food cooked with maize powder, greens and kidney beans), and *borde* are what they can afford and easily consume. *Injera* and accompanying sauces will be consumed with *gomen* (*aloko*) and *shiro* (bean sauce), but these are consumed not regularly. This combination can be eaten more or less in a day according to the foods they have on hand in the house and their purchasing power. The combinations of food consumed in a day are shown in Figure 2.6, drawn from interviews in Kebelle A.

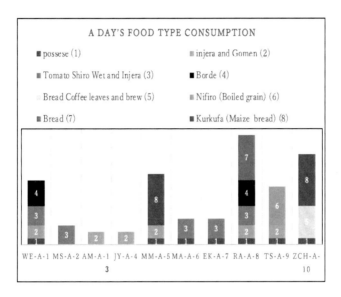

Figure 2.6: One day food type consumption by household

2.5.4.4   *Risk management*

Diversifying their livelihood mix and income source is one way of buil ding their livelihood for the future. Local people in Kebelle A are engaged in a number of activities to diversify their income opportunity. This are e ngaged in food and beverage business, e.g., food and spice preparation, bor -de making, and teal making (a grain-based beer like drink). Usually, a hou- sehold will be engaged in one of the activities as their main livelihood, f- or example, areke making, but in order to diversify their income base they will also engage in more than one activity. The system, however, is highly regulated in such a way that every woman will have a set date to sell he r product so that competition is avoided. This also reflects the fact that th e number of consumers is limited in the village.

2.5.4.5   Tourist cash as a means to address vulnerability—livelihood diversification

Households in Kebelle A engage in tourism as one strategy to curb livelihood vulnerability. As can be seen in Table 2.2, households mix strategies. Out of the 11 households, 6 cultivate plots of land between 0.25 ha and 0.5 ha in area. Their plot size is considered small; however, they are better off than those who do not have any. Four of the eleven are female-headed households that do not own land and must depend on their small businesses, along with tourism.

Table 2.2: Livelihood strategy mix in Kebelle A

Household	Cultivatio	Areke	Pottery	Injera	Metalsmith	Borde Mk.	Room Rent	City work	Teaching	Fix mud hus.	F. wood selling	Tourism	Tourist Incom range	Food	Utensils	Borde	Iqub	Gomen/mabaya	Coffee	Chicken/feast
WE-1*	0											0	100-30	0	0	0	0			
MS-2		0										0	1000-30					0		
AM-3*		0	0	0								0	100-30	0						
GA-4	0	0						0	0			0	30					0		
MM-5	0					0	0					0	2000-30					0		
MA-6	0										0	0	100-30					0	0	
EK-7*		0				0						0	100-30					0		
RA-8	0	0										0	50-30					0		
TS-9	0	0										0	20-30					0		
Zch-10	0	0	0						0			0	200		0			0		
AA-11*		0								0	0	0	100-30	0				0		0

In Kebelle A, income from tourism activity is a means to close the gap. During an interview on tourist cash as benefit, one participant stated,

> ... for us satisfaction from tourist earning is just that it covers the day's need, it does not mean that we have accomplished what we aspire to in life. (M. M.)

Cash earned from tourists is often spent on food items (Figure 2.7), which are the priority items as a result all respondents respondents report that their cash from tourist is utilized to purchase food and condiments, accompaniments mabaya; and beverages such as coffee and borde. This is all 11 households interviewed reported using all or most of their cash for food items. When earnings are substantial, local people in Kebelle A said that they use cash for other needs, especially strengthening their business. During interviews with household members, the minimum and maximum tourist earnings reported range from 25 ETB ($0.97) to 1000 ETB ($36) in one visit. Tourist cash is highly seasonal.

2.6   Access to cash and capitalizing women's capability

As members of an agrarian community, women in Kebelle A are usually engaged in farming along with their husbands, in addition to their daily gender roles, fetching water, firewood, child bearing, household chores, etc. In addition to these tasks, women also engage in small business activities to improve their livelihood. As a result, women in Kebelle A engage in *areke* making and/or *borde* making to gain extra cash, even those whose main livelihood is cultivation or whose husbands work in the city or as civil servants in the local government.

Thus, tourism activity in Kebelle A provides an additional option for diversifying their livelihood mix. As a result, in Kebelle A, as in all the other Kebelles where the tourist initiative operates, the majority participating are women, except for the metalsmiths. In Kebelle A, of the 11 households, 10 are headed by women. These women report that any extra cash when in good amount is spent on their business, to pay for their *iqub*, or to buy input for their business.

> *I usually want to save what I get from the tourists to improve my business. That does not happen a lot, what we get is often not much, so I use it for daily needs; that is also good. (E.K. 2017)*

The women in the neighborhood, who are not even in the initiative have been stimulated to start some kind of business to attract tourists. Those who make *areke* are often those that get visits. Therefore, the women are starting to produce *areke,* but the guide association has thus far stuck to their main group members. Still, they anticipate that at one point the tourists will come and visit them.

Tourist activities in Kebelle A give women the opportunity to showcase what they do and capitalize their capabilities. Tourists come to visit only to see what they do as their everyday activity. This does not add any extra burden on the women, and since the initiative offers a favorable opportunity to make extra cash, most women wish to participate.

2.7   Life story: The story of E.K. in Kebelle A

E.K. is my host in Kebelle A. E.K. said she was four years old when she moved from the Bench Maji area, far to the west across the Omo River.

Her mother with three of her siblings moved to Ari in the 1990s due to conflicts with a neighboring ethnic group, the Mursi/Suri, in which her father was killed during a cattle raid. This was during the time of change from the Derg to the currently ruling EPRDF. She said that the conflict started because the vacuum of administration allowed people to loot and raid neighboring villages during the transition. Her mother raised three children alone, two sisters and an elder brother. Her mother made a living making *areke* and carrying wood from the nearby cure forest adjacent to the Mago National Park to sell in the market. The Ari people were welcoming, she said, so they settled there and have remained ever since.

E.K. said that her life's aspiration was diminished during her childhood. When she was ready to go to school she enrolled in the nearby elementary school with her elder brother. However, they never had enough to eat at home, so she was always hungry. She could not remain in school, but her brother was strong enough to bear it, so he continued. She joined her mother to help her in her *areke* making, collecting wood for sale and for the business. After three years she went back to school, but her brother was three grades ahead of her. While in school she was abducted at the age of fifteen and taken to Addis Ababa without her consent. She still thinks that it was due to witchcraft. Once she came to her senses she begged to go back home and returned to her family. This also became the fate of her younger sister at the age of fifteen, in 2016. This saddens E.K. to this day.

E.K. then moved to the Omo National Park to work as a cook in the newly constructed sugar factory. Many often encouraged her to go back to school while she was young. After a few years she saved some money and returned home in 2008, started her own business making *areke*, and went back to school. She went to school full time (schools run for half a day) and worked the rest of the time on her *areke* business.

In 2011 she met her daughter's father and had S. He was an agricultural college student at the time. Once he got a job in another woreda he left and did not come back to the family. She had to go to court to get child support to raise her daughter.

She lives as a single mother in a rented house with her six-year-old daughter. She makes her living with her *areke* making and says that life is difficult. At the time she was going to school full time and attending tenth grade. She took the final exam in 2018; however, her results were not good enough to get her into a college.

She sells her *areke* to a retailer in the village, who gives her a better deal than taking it to the nearest market. After school, E.K. spends all her time preparing and organizing her input for her *areke* business. She has to collect firewood from the nearby forest on a daily basis, which takes one to two hours round trip. She said that scarcity of fuel wood in the nearby forest is making her trip longer by the day. Farmland encroachment and land for expanding buildings from the nearby city of Jinka is pushing the forest cover ever further from her village. Buying firewood would be too expensive for her, given her limited income. As the nearest water point is out of order, she also has to collect river water for her business and all her needs at home. Otherwise, she would have to purchase water as well.

2.7.1   Tourist cash as an additional income

She said that the Ari guide association approached her to participate in the tourist visit initiative that they organized. She was very happy to be part of the scheme. She hopped that some extra cash from tourists would make a difference. Tourists come and visit her work, try *areke,* and sometimes buy half a litter bottle of *areke* for ETB50 ($1.80). The flow of tourists is good, she said; however, the guides are not consistent in settling the amount of money she earns according to their deal. She said that she has to chase them all the time to get the money due her. For her, any extra money she can get, however meager, covers a gap. She said that it is a good opportunity, as she does not have to engage in any extra activity since they come to see what she normally does every day, so the cash is extra income that she cannot ignore.

We calculated E.K.'s income and expenditures for one week to see what she earned from her main activities. Her total weekly expenditure of 1,357 birr ($59.00) is greater than her total weekly income of 1,219 birr ($53.00). E.K. is thus operating at a loss. I went to the local market to check the prices of all the inputs for *areke* and *borde* against the quotations she gave me. Except for a few variations, the prices she provided were consistent. She was not surprised, she said: "I am toiling, still it does not add up…sometimes I am just working for nothing." That week there was only one tourist visit. They were two people, and the guide gave her 30 ETB.

2.7.2   *Reflections on her life story*

E.K.'s life was one of turmoil at an early age, war, and displacement, with a new beginning in a far country after she lost her father, and when she was young at school, the challenges persisted. Not having enough to eat forced her to drop out of school. She believes that changed her life course when her brother was better able to continue his school, as he is now a government employee who leads a better life. Her struggle continued as she was abducted at an early age, divorced, and left as a single mother. She engages in a trade that she is familiar with, making *areke*, which she learned from her mother, to survive. Still, the effort she puts in is not enough due to her limited access to water and firewood for her consumption and her business.

She sought tourist cash as an opportunity to change her life, but she says it is also a struggle. The guide association that introduced the scheme is not trustworthy in handing her due benefit from tourist encounter.

2.7.3   *E. K.'s day in Kebelle A (Friday, September 2017)*

E.K. is up early at 6 am, as always. She said, "*Areke itidalehu*," I will set the pots to distill *areke* today. She has already set up four fireplaces with pots. She has 160 liters of fermented sludge to distill. This involved 65 kg of maize, 4 kg of mixed grain (sorghum, wheat, barley, millet) to be sprouted and made into flour, 5 kg of hops, up to 10 jerry cans of 25 liters of water, and four to five bundles of fuel wood, of which about two she will buy, and the rest she will bring from the nearest forest. This will produce 24 liters of *Areke.*

As she was preparing to set her pots, someone shouted that one of the communal tap water points was open for her to collect water, so she ran to it with a 25-liter jerry can. As she was running off, she said for me to use the water to wash my clothes, for she would have water for her work. I started to wash my clothes. About 20 minutes later she came back and said they had closed the water point and she was not able to bring water. I felt bad as I had used the scarce water. I started to minimize the amount I was using to leave some for-house use. Right after that, they again shouted that they had opened the other water point, so she ran again to collect water. This time she was successful in filling up her 25-liter jerry can for the day.

Once she returned from the water point, she continued with her *areke* distillation process. In *areke* distillation, the process requires filling up pots with fermented sledge (Photo 2.7) and stirring it, and once it starts to boil, she tightly covers the pots for the distillation to proceed. Once the distillation process is over, she collects her *areke* from the little container, *bilki*, to pour it into a jerry can. She pours out the sledge from the pot, which once cooled can be given to the cattle as feed. Usually, she gives it to the neighborhood and barters for firewood, after which she will again fill the pots for another round of distillation.

As she carried on her distillation, on the side, she prepared coffee and invited her neighbors to drink coffee with us. This is a normal procedure in the village whereby each house takes its turn during the day to prepare coffee, and they all invite each other over and drink it together. As we were having our coffee, she gave her daughter her breakfast, a leftover from last night: *injera* with some bean sauce. All the children playing with her daughter also joined her to eat with her. Her daughter, however, was unhappy with the food from the night before, so she started crying and did not want to eat. Her friends continued eating without her without any complaint.

After the coffee, E.K. started to prepare for her borde drink (another grain-based drink), which she is going to sell on Monday, which is her turn once every week in the village. Each woman has one day per week to sell borde. E.K. said this was in order to avoid unnecessary competition and spoiling their drink. To start the fermentation, mix of maize and sorghum flour, she cooked it to make a porridge-like paste, let it cool, and mixed it with sprouted barley flour to increase the fermentation rate of the mix. The next day, she told me, she would make porridge of more maize and barley flour, let it cool, and mix it with the fermented mix. That will be left overnight and will be ready to drink the next day as borde. To make her borde, she used 10 kg of maize and sorghum flour, and 1 ½ kg of sprouted barley flour for the fermentation.

Photo 2.7: Pouring fermented mix into the distillation pots

In between she will tend to her *areke* distillation. The processes of *areke* distillation continued until it was dark, around 7 pm in the evening. As the kitchen does not have lighting she had to stop and continue the next day.

That day there were no tourist visits, nor the next day. A tourist visit, by two young Israelis, only occurred on Tuesday.

2.8   The effect of cultural tourism on wellbeing in Kebelle A

A participatory wellbeing evaluation was conducted during the FGD in an attempt to allow local people to come up with their own indicators to measure wellbeing against the level of benefit from tourist income. Participants listed indicators to describe the state of wellbeing in their perspective. For the wellbeing indicator, they were asked to indicate the state of good life, *mitchu hiwot* in Amharic or *dokintoiyo uste* in Ari; as all participants were bilingual, we needed the term in both Ari and Amharic.

According to the FGD participants in Kebelle A, they put wellbeing in three categories: the first good life dokintiyo *uste/michu hiwot*,   and described by the level of production of grain at a household level—at a rough estimation up to 50 –100kg of maize, with the type of food consumed being a staple food type made from *teff* (Eragrostis tef)   preparing a pancake like bread   *teff ingera asmi–gashi balchi* , cattle *waki* (30), and goats *darte* (40; Table 2.3). They will have good health and their family will be educated. They have savings and are involved in *iqub* and *iddir*; they own their house, *aya*, and assets in the house such as a television and music recorder, a wooden arm chair, and utensils; and they will have a good network of people—good contacts are important to make it in life, as was stated during the FGD.

The second indicator is *mers lekmyo*, which is a medium level of wellbeing. In this category life is not as comfortable as the first, but they have the necessary basic needs. They have to purchase from the market, consume maize *injera* as *teff* is expensive, and they may own their hut or rent a home, and have a few livestock: 3 cattle and 5 goats; not many household goods, only owning a wooden stool, *cursi*; a good family base, some contacts to get them by in life; they are members of the local *iddir*; involved in the local saving scheme *iqub*; and their family is going to school and they are in good health (Table 2.2).

The third category, *kin tstskiye*, in Amharic *yaltemmuala hiwot*, an unfulfilled life. Life in which they have no production of their own, so they purchase grain or food from the market. Mostly dependent on others, *ed eare gura asude*; may rent a house, but mostly dependent, *ed kikn esmti.* The type of food can be *dodere* (taro); *nifiro* (boiled grain); *posessi* (maize flour cooked with vegetables). They do not have cattle or small ruminants like goats. This category of people does not have membership in the *iddir* or join the *iqub*, as their disposable income is limited. They find it hard for their family to go to school and often are not in good health. In general, they are described as being in destitution—*guskulina* (Amharic word).

2.8.1   *Rating the benefits from tourist income on wellbeing indicators*

Participants of the FGD were asked to compare the benefit they receive from tourists to the kind of wellbeing they have now and what they expect by rating the benefit from tourism on a scale of 0–10. The group, after a thorough discussion, rated the benefit from tourism at 3. They said that although the income is minimal, it still adds to their life needs. The blame for a low level of benefit from tourism is placed on the working modalities, which are not clear and transparent: *giltse aserar yelem*, *metemamen yelem*, there is no trust between the guides and themselves, and now the conflicts between the young men in their neighborhood are creating a much worse scenario where the guide association *Akimi le negew sew* is avoiding the site for fear of the conflict. In between, the local people who used to benefit from tourism are losing.

2.9   Perception of overall wellbeing/life satisfaction in Kebelle A

The quantitative exercise to measure perception of overall wellbeing/life satisfaction in Kebelle A involved 51 purposefully selected individuals and was undertaken to determine the perceptions of local people regarding their overall life satisfaction/wellbeing in the villages that are engaged in tourism activities. For this exercise we included respondents from three of the other villages that are involved in the tourism sector within the same initiative. Thirteen questions were categorized into four life satisfaction domains: Material Wellbeing, Community Wellbeing, Emotional Wellbeing, and Health and Safety Wellbeing. The Likert scale had five possible responses, *highly dissatisfied* (1), *not satisfied* (2), *moderate* (3), *satisfied* (4), and *highly satisfied* (5). As a result, the overall life satisfaction/QOL of each person's aggregated responses to all 13 questions was taken as the mean score (Figure 2.7) to show the tendency of the life satisfaction of all 51 respondents. According to this calculation the average mean for Kebele A is 3.

This means that the average tendency of perception of people in Kebelle A reflects a moderate life satisfaction in the Likert scale survey.

2.9.1   *Material wellbeing (economic QOL)*

In this category, the responses on basic needs (food, shelter, and clothing) and level of income from tourism showed that the majority of respondents considered themselves "not satisfied" with their basic needs and income level from tourism. This is consistent with their qualitative exercise on the value of the benefit from tourism.

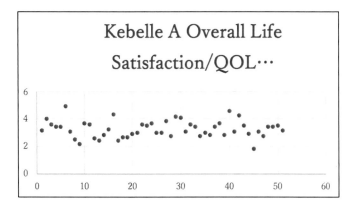

Figure 2.7: Perception of overall life satisfaction/QOL mean score in Kebelle A

Table 2.3: Participatory wellbeing indicators in Kebelle A

Indicators	Wellbeing Categories		
	Category 1	Category 2	Category 3
	dokintiyo ste/mitchu (good life)	*mers lekmyo* (Moderate quality of life)	*tsoskinda (kin tstskiye) yaltemuala hiwot* (Destitution)
Food quality and quantity	50 (100ks) – rough estimate; *teff injera-galshi balchi*	Upto 10 (100kgs); Maize *injera – fiter balshi*	Grain purchased; *godere, Nifro, possesi*
Housing	Own – *korkoro bet*	Hut – owned/rented	Rent/dependent ed *eare gura asude*
Assets			
- Livestock	Cattle *waki* 30; goat *darte* 40	Cattle 3; goat 5	-
- Household goods	Sofa, TV, Music player	wooden stool *cursi*	-
Family life	Extended family	Some family members	Not good
Social Network	Good network, *iddir* member	Some contacts; *iddir* member	Not member of *iddir*
Savings	*iquib* member	*iquib* member	Not *iquib* member
Education	Family schooled	Family schooled	-
Health	In good status	In good status	Not well

Kebelle, A. wellbeing indictors

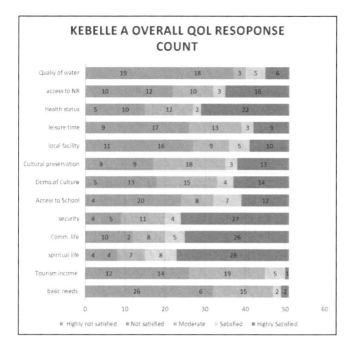

Figure 2.8: Perception of QOL responses in Kebelle A

2.9.2   *Community wellbeing and emotional wellbeing (social and cultural QOL)*

For community wellbeing and emotional wellbeing, comprising eight Likert-scored items in all, local people's responses were "satisfied." These shows that their social assets keep the local people satisfied, compensating for their lack in material wellbeing. This was evident especially regarding their satisfaction with community life, their security level, and their spiritual life. According to respondents, their spiritual life has provided them comfort by removing and abolishing caste-based discrimination and ensured their worth in their community.

2.9.3   *Health and safety domain (environmental QOL)*

In this category of life satisfaction, there are three Likert-scored items. Response counts reflect their complaints about access to clean water, which showed that the majority were not satisfied with the quality of water or access to natural resources, such as the dwindling forest cover and urbanization mentioned before that are pushing their main resources further away.

2.10   Four impacts of tourism: economic, social, cultural, and environmental

As part of the life satisfaction scale, the impact of tourism on four factors: economy, social, cultural, and environmental, was added to assess local people's perception of the impact of tourism. As a result, responses on the Likert scale were categorized as *strongly disagree* (1), *disagree* (2), *not sure* (3), *agree* (4), and *strongly agree* (5).

The response counts are shown in Figure 2.9 under total impact response (see detailed responses for each element under Annex V.A.1–7).

2.10.1   The economic impact of tourism

Regarding responses on the economic impact of tourism, the majority of respondents disagreed that tourism improved the standard of living and created an opportunity for income (Figure 2.9). This is comparable with the low level of the benefit from tourism reported on the qualitative exercise.

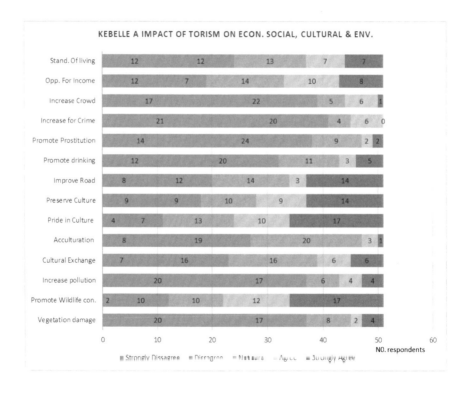

Figure 2.9: Perception of toursim impact response count, Kebelle A

2.10.2   *The social and cultural impacts of tourism*

A majority of respondents did not believe that tourism has a negative impact socially, that is, it does not promote drinking or prostitution, nor does it increase crime or crowds. However, some people did not believe that tourism improved road access. They say that the road that was created has not improved at all. It is still the same as in the beginning, not even tarmacked. Regarding its cultural impact, the majority of local people believe that tourism has a positive impact on culture, in terms of increasing pride in the culture and preserving cultural assets. However, they expressed a high level of disagreement with the statement that tourism promotes cultural exchange, for they said that as they do not have any cultural exchange with tourists, there is no exchange. Finally, for the item on acculturation as a negative impact of tourism on culture, respondents disagreed that tourism has an effect on acculturation in their area.

2.10.3   *The environmental impact of tourism*

A majority of respondents disagreed that tourists have a negative impact on the environment through damage to the vegetation cover, but agreed that tourism has a positive impact on wildlife conservation. They pointed to the creation of the Mago National Park as an example.

2.11   Conclusion

This chapter has examined a cultural tourism scenario in a peri-urban setting in South Ari, SOZ. This tourism scenario is a newer initiative than tourism activities within the Zone that was started by a local youth guide association to create new activities for tourists coming to the zone to visit established tourist destinations among the lowland pastoral communities. The initiative targets local households who are already engaged in small local artisanal businesses, including small food and beverage businesses and metalsmiths in four villages in Jinka, the zonal town of SOZ. The majority of participating households are headed by women engaged in small food and beverage businesses, apart from the metalsmith. The tourists visit households engaged in different activities that are already the local peoples' daily activities.

Tourists can also be given the chance to participate in such tasks as baking *injera* or testing the type of food or drink. In this regard, local people's cultural asset, which is already their livelihood strategy, is an additional opportunity to diversify their cash income. According to the local people, cash earned from the initiative creates a means of coping with vulnerable situations.

However, the ways of working and benefit sharing with the guide association lacks trust and transparency. The local group complained that, although a good flow of tourists exist, payment from the visits is not passed to them completely as agreed, mostly because this type of business transaction is on an informal basis and local authorities that heavily regulate the guide association have no direct contact with or knowledge of the final destination where the tourist interest is based. As a result, the local people feel powerless, neglected, excluded, and to an extent exploited. Still, they continue to participate for fear of losing the opportunity altogether, for local people say that however meagre the income is from the initiative, it still constitutes valuable input into their livelihood. As a result, they continue to engage in tourism in anticipation of some correction of the transaction.

The tourist initiative has created access to supplementary income for some of the women of Kebelle A by capitalizing on the capabilities and local knowledge that already constitute their means of livelihood. As a result, it helps them diversify their income without additional effort, thus interesting more women in the village to engage in it in order to earn extra cash.

The results of a participatory wellbeing valuation and a Likert-scored questionnaire showed comparatively similar scores on a scale of 0 to 10 to the perception of quality of life, which showed an overall mean score of 3, indicating moderate satisfaction. In this regard, it can be said that cultural tourism has not yet provided sufficient quality of life/wellbeing for people in Kebelle A. It is however understood that the people who receive any amount of cash from the tourist consider it valuable, as it gives relief to their vulnerable livelihood. This may show the level of vulnerability in their livelihood. The local people feel that it has the potential to provide alternative means to substantiate their livelihood; however, they feel that they are missing such opportunities because of the mistrust and lack of transparency in the initiative. They are holding discussions to try to improve the situation by setting an entrance fee for all tourists c to pay before they start their visit; this amount is to be paid directly to the villages. The amount they agreed on during the FGD is ETB20/person ($0.036). This is not much, but it will give them slightly better benefits than what they are getting now, especially when larger groups come to visit.

As a local initiative, the activity is unique in the area, perhaps even in the country. However, it will require some corrections regarding benefit sharing, transparency, and trust building among the local people. The style of engaging tourists can also be taken as innovative in the area and can be spread, as it presents a good approach by introducing the local culture, increasing the pride of the local people, and showcasing their capabilities.

CHAPTER3

THE CULTURAL TOURISM SCENARIO IN MURSILAND

3.1   Introduction

This chapter will overview the cultural tourism scenario in one of SOZ's most popular tourist destinations. According to the local informants, tourists have been visiting Mursiland since the 1970s. However, historical records of outside visitors, including travelers and explorers, entering the area date back to the late 19th century. All the informants in the area today state that tourists come to the region through the attraction of the local people and culture, although the area has two major protected national parks, the Omo National Park and the Mago National Park.

This chapter will provide a brief overview of the people in Mursiland, followed by a detailed discussion of its tourism scenario from a cultural context. It will also highlight the main livelihood pattern and the challenges identified by previous researchers, and mainly elaborate on the cultural asset that has created an opportunity for local people in Mursiland to address vulnerabilities in their livelihood, as per the local people's accounts. Cash from tourists is highly sought to improve their financial security; it acts as an alternative financial source to selling their livestock.

It also discusses how local women gain access to and control over cash to address their daily needs. This chapter will also present the result of a participatory wellbeing indicator identification exercise and a Likert-scale survey of the perceptions of local people of their quality of life and the impact of tourism on its economic, social, cultural, and environmental elements.

3.1.1   *Background*

Mursiland is located in the lower Omo Valley, Salamago Woreda (district). It is one of the six tourist destinations in the total of eight woredas in SOZ. The people from Mursiland identify themselves as "Mun." Outsiders use the term Mursi to address the locals, identified as "Mun," with "Muni" singular (LaTosky, 2013). The Mursi belong to the Nilo-Saharan, Eastern Sudanic group. According to the latest official census (CSA, 2008a, 2008b), the population in Mursiland is

7,500 in an area of 2,000 km², but most believe that the population today exceeds 10,000 people. In the strip of land between two rivers, the Omo in the west and south and the Mago in the east, the Mursi depend on two types of cultivation and livestock for their livelihood. The territory ranges between 500–1000m above sea level, with vegetation cover predominantly of bush belts and wooded grasslands that maintain their livelihood of rain-fed cultivation and animal herding (Turton, 1988).

Early records show that colonial expeditions, comprising geographical and military expeditions, big game hunting groups, and surveys performing the triangulation of international border markers in Eastern Africa, entered into the territory at the end of the nineteenth century (Turton, 1981). According to Turton (1988), the first geographical explorers, Samuel Teleki and Ludwig Von Hohenl, identified the Mursi ethnic group for the first time, along with all other groups in the Lower Omo Valley; and Vittorio Bottego, an Italian explorer, described the Mursi in detail along with their ancestors and their neighboring groups in the year 1896. Turton (1981) noted that Bottego, accompanied by Emperor Menelik's troops during his exploration at the time, stated that the Mursi identified people from the North as Kuchumba, as is the case today. Emperor Menelik's expansion efforts in the territory were successful in 1909 after a border settlement with the British in East Africa that marked the whole of the Lower Omo Valley, including Mursiland, as being within the territory of Ethiopia as delineated by a surveyor, C. W. Gwynn (Turton, 1981).

Numerous linguists and anthropologists began to study the Omo Valley languages and cultures starting in the 1960s and early 1970s. Much of what we know about the Mursiland today has been through the anthropological work of David Turton, an anthropologist, since the late 1960s.

In the mid-1960s, conservation programs were introduced in the Lower Omo valley by an expert, Lasely Brown, which led to the formation of the Omo National Park in 1966, later taken up by two other experts, John Stephenson and Akinori Mizuno, in 1978 (Adams & Hutton, 2007). At both times, the conservation programs' focus has excluded the local people who were the rightful inhabitants of the area (LaTosky, 2013; Nishizaki, 2014; Turton, 2003). The idea was to totally evict the people to form a vast protected area to attract tourists and revenue for the state, with the demarcation of a total land area of 8,348 km² for three Wildlife Protected Areas (WPA), the Omo, Mago, and Tama WPAs, which are registered as "The Mega Biodiversity Complex" (Ethiopian Wildlife Conservation Authority, 2011). The local people still have to fight state coercion to maintain their livelihood, which has been highly dependent on the natural resources within this demarcated space for centuries. The scheme's failure to consult the relevant ethnic groups in the area has created resentment until today, beyond depriving the group of their prime land for their livelihood and social function (Adams & Hutton, 2007; LaTosky, 2013; Turton 2003, 2013).

Right about the same time, the Mursi had also to face external shocks that threatened their subsistence livelihood. According to Turton (1986), the Mursi livelihood has been recorded as subsistence with occasional hungry times. However, this turned severe with devastating and deadly famine after a series of failed rains for three consecutive years in 1971, 1972, and 1973, and reduced floods on the river beds.

During the Derg era and military rule, hardship continued after a short improvement of the situation. Drought occurred again in 1977, which led the Mursi to migrate northward in 1979 to better-watered land in the Mago Valley at the foot of Mt. Mago (1176m above sea level; Turton, 1986). At the time, the move was said to take some of them away from their flood retreat cultivation on the Omo river bed but placed them with a better opportunity for rain-fed cultivation. Moreover, the move put them close to a nearby weekly market where they could sell their produce and in bad years purchase grain and sell their cattle. According to Turton (1985, 2005), that was a defining time in the history of the Mursi regarding how they respond naturally to serious ecological pressures and exercise their adaptive capacity.

In the early 1990s, the Omo River was identified as the main potential source of hydropower for the country, the Gibe, in its upper basin (Turton, 2010). As a result, starting in 2004, Gibes I, II, and II were constructed, with the last project being finished in 2016. This was said to have a negative effect on the size of annual Omo flood, which is important for all the ethnic groups along the river Omo that are engaged in flood retreat cultivation, a type of cultivation that utilizes the silt after a river flood has subsided.

At the beginning of the 1990s, large-scale agricultural schemes intensified as a means of economic development. This policy, part of the second Growth and Transformation Program (GTP II) in 2015, accompanied a villagization program (Towelde & Fana, 2014) to resettle people from the demarcated areas. This move, for economic development, claiming to fully utilize the Omo River and change the pastoral community's precarious life along the River Omo, led to a further appropriation of 175,000 ha of land for the state-owned Sugar Corporation. The area is part of the total land appropriated at the national level, a total of 365,000 ha, including large-scale agricultural acquisition schemes (Strecker, 2014; Towelde & Fana, 2014).

This move has another dimension, as economic development is expected to profoundly change the demographics of the area. According to an interview respondent in Jinka (2018) operating in Nyangatom and research conducted by the EU (2016), a huge influx of a labor force of 400,000–700,000 individuals from the highlands is moving to work in the sugarcane plantations in Salamago and Nyangatom Woredas, which are the least densely populated in the zone (8.33% and 8.77% respectively), as compared to the densest woredas of Ari, which range between 166.87–318.64. This is feared that it may reduce indigenous communities to making up less than ten %of the Wereda population (EU, 2016). This can also impact the acculturation of the local indigenous population.

Furthermore, the zone's precarious situation continues today with research indicating that the adverse impacts of climate change and variability, particularly in pastoralist and agro-pastoralist areas, affect livestock productivity (Eneyew, 2015; Suryabhagavan, 2016).

3.2   The livelihood pattern in Mursiland

The Mursi are divided into five territorially based groups/constituencies, the *bhurayoga*, that enable them to control access to pasture land and water in Mursiland (Turton, 1979, 2004). The region is divided horizontally from north to south into three large groups: the Dola, consisting of the Baruba, Mogujo, and Bigolokare; the Arioli; and the Gongulobibi. All groups have access to the full range of natural resources, from flood land in the east to dry season grazing land in the west.

The Mursi are transhumant, partially moving to and from places in need of pasture and water for livestock (Turton, 1995). Administratively, the Mursi territory is divided into four Kebelles, Makki, Hayiloha ("Megento" to the Mursi), Moizo, and Bongozo, in Mursiland. Hayiloha is situated in the central part of the Mursi territory, where the only all-weather-road crossing from Jinka Town in the east through Mago National Park towards the Omo River and Sugar Factory No. 2 in the west. This road is also the main access road for tourists into Mursi territory.

As agro-pastoralists, the Mursi depend predominantly on two types of grain cultivation and livestock rearing. Grain makes up 70% of their food intake, for which they have no substitute (Turton, 1986). Sorghum and maize are the main cultivars, except for some forest greens they include as an accompaniment to consume with their porridge *tila* and milk. The second main livelihood system is livestock rearing, which makes up 20% of their food intake (Turton, 1986). Women are the main cultivators, and men look after the livestock.

3.2.1   *Rain-fed cultivation*

The rain-fed agriculture season, *Oioyi*, is during the heavy rains in March–April, with harvests in June–July called the *Telagai*. According to Turton (2004), rainfall patterns are highly unreliable, with an average of 480mm. The rain-fed cultivation of hoe-farming and shifting cultivation, where they slash and burn a forested area to obtain fertile soil rather than plowing, uses a minimum tillage of the land for a number of years (2–4) until it is considered infertile. The land then is left to regrow to recover its forest cover and fertility. In June–August after the harvest, *Telagai* is the time of plenty and social occasions, if a good harvest year.

Photo 3.1: Rain-fed cultivation preparation

Photo 3.2: Flood retreat cultivation

3.2.2   Flood retreat cultivation

The flood retreat cultivation season, the *Lour*, starts in January–February after the small rains in October–November. This cultivation happens on the banks of the Omo and Mago Rivers within Mursi territory.

After the flood retreats, fertile soil remaining on the riverbanks is used to cultivate maize and sorghum. This type of cultivation along the Omo River is now diminishing due to appropriation of the Omo riverbank to build five state-owned sugar factories. This means that groups close to the Omo River have abandoned *Lour* cultivation, so only those who are near and around rivers Mago *makki* and *elma* only continue with rain-fed cultivation .

3.2.3   Livestock rearing

According to Turton (1995), both cultivations are insufficient to meet all food needs. As a result, livestock has been a critical source of food in the form of milk products, but more so as they constitute insurance in a time of harsh years when produce from the two cultivations is not sufficient. The towns of Hnka and Hana are the nearest markets to purchase grain at times of crop failure. Livestock is thus important to raise cash in time of external shocks such as rain variability or pests that lead to crop failure.

3.3   Basic local services in Mursiland

Hayiloha or *megento* was a central village where the official government structures were situated. In the village of Megento, there was a school, a health post, an animal health post, a small museum, and a water point until recently as dilapidated structures of the buildings can be seen. All these are now abandoned because of an internal conflict between the local people and the administration.

Hanna is the seat of Salamago Woreda. A 2018 visit to the woreda administration office provided some basic information on the general situation in Mursiland.

The local administrative official revealed during the interview that basic services in Mursiland are limited. This is due to limited road access into the Kebelles. In principle, he said, facilities should be up and running, and those that have been built earlier are out of order now. The other difficulty in the area is the issue of security, as the conflict between the local people and local authority persists even to this day.

The local authority said that local people are constantly requesting facilitation of tourists' road access to reach their Kebelles. The tourists are currently only visiting one Kebelle, Haıl-Wha, which is intersected by the main access road from Jinka to the Omo River. Beyond that, tourists do not make any attempt to enter the villages as the poor situation of the roads leaves them inaccessible. Travel agencies and local guides are not willing to take tourists further even if the type of vehicles used for their trip are to some extent able to make trips beyond the villages close to the roadside. The office claimed limited capacity to increase road access. At the same time, issues of security and conflict are hindering accessibility. In order to alleviate this problem, they plan to work closely with the local people. At the moment, the woreda is planning to engage researchers to work on peace, security, and conflict resolution issues in the area.

3.3.1   *The campaign against harmful traditional practices (HTP)*

One main concern for the office is harmful traditional practices (HTP) against which they would like to organize training for local people. This campaign has been going on since 2008, and the main aim is to create awareness among the local people of certain cultural practices to be abandoned as harmful. During an interview (February 2019), the expert said that they do not worry about the impact of tourism or the threat on the local culture or cultural acculturation; rather, their worry is how to create awareness of harmful traditional practices among the local people.

3.3.2   *Zonal level interventions*

Based on a document review of the zonal six-month (2018–2019) project implementation report, programs implemented within the woreda include activities such as awareness-raising on issues like harmful traditional practices, conflict resolution, and benefits of villagization. Villagization in Mursi is intended to congregate agro-pastoral households within a five-kilometer radius into one village, where water, health, education, animal health, agricultural extension, and other benefits are provided. In Mursiland, a total of 148 households were planned to be villagized within the reported period, but the success rate was nil. A zonal representative said that they are aware of the tendency of the local people, but the hope is that they will gradually take up the scheme and utilize the services provided.

A visit to one of the villages in the north, Makki Kebelle, demonstrated a huge land set up with facilities such as a mill, health post, water point, animal health post, etc., but no people were residing in the place. A key informant in the area explained that the mill was very important for the people; however, it is now out of order. Still, the report reveals that more facilities are being constructed in 2019.

Among other activities reported at the zonal level, a regional initiative, the Regional Pastoralist Livelihood Development Project (RPLRP), supported by the Intergovernmental Authority on Development (IGAD), an eight-country trade bloc in Africa, the World Bank, and the local government is operating in three agro-pastoralist woredas within the zone, namely, Nyangatom, Dassenech, and Hamer woredas, but not in Mursiland. An EU commissioned report also indicates that among 31 civil society/non-governmental organizations (NGOs) operating in the zone, only three are in Salamago Woreda, where Mursiland is situated. One missionary organization, the Sudanese Interior Mission (SIM), located in Makki Kebelle, has been providing health, education, and animal health facilities for many years (EU, 2016).

This research observation also showed that there was a huge piece of land under development for agriculture as part of the villagization scheme in the north of Mursiland, the Makki area, through the Zonal Pastoralist Affairs Department, to prepare 267 hectares of land with 6 km of irrigation canal development and land of 0.5 ha/household to be handed over to each household when it moves into the settlement area.

3.4   Cultural tourism in Mursiland

Mursiland is one of the major cultural tourist destinations in the zone and very popular internationally. Lip cutting and the lip plate, *dhebinya tugony*, of women and girls are the significant features drawing tourists to Mursiland. Girls cut their lips at 15 after they have had their first period, and gradually insert clay plates up to 30 cm in diameter. Lip cutting is a Mursi girl's transitioning ritual into adulthood (LaTosky, 2009; Turton, 2004), signifying sexual maturity and beauty. It is also their mark of identity as it distinguishes them from their neighbors, thus creating a livelihood opportunity through tourism as their cultural asset.

3.4.1   *Accounts of early visitors in Mursiland*

A senior Mursi elder recalls that the Mursi's first tourist came about 39 years ago through the Omo River, around 1969. A local elder, a senior tourism officer, also recalls that tourist visits started after the existing access road was made following the establishment of the Mago National Park (MNP) by the local people in 1973 through a food-for-work scheme. The main interest of tourists at the time was, however, the people in Mursiland. A young man who started as a guide and who now runs his own travel and tour company in Jinka said,

> In 1997, the Mursi were shy, tourists were Dub ida… sudden, unexpected visitors—so they run when they see tourists whom they call haranchi. In the late 80s, they start interacting, and tourists started to give 1 ETB ($0.125) to the Mursi for their photos. Today they receive 5–10 ETB ($0.180–$0.360).

3.4.2   *Photos for cash—the tourist scenario in Mursiland*

As in most tourist destinations in South Omo, tourism in Mursi is limited to a "photos for cash" scenario, where the local people in Mursi are involved in a transaction of cash from tourists for photos of lip cut/plated Mursi girls and women. Children and men also participate in the exercise, earning money along the way. In some instances, the sale by women of artifacts such as clay lip plates and leather capes add to their cash earnings.

Tourists can only enter Mursiland with guides from the zone, who are paid 400 ETB ($14). As the Mursi territory is located beyond the Mago National Park (MNP), the tourists have to pay an entrance fee of MNP and scout service of 435ETB ($16)/person and a car fee of 80ETB ($3), which is collected by the regional government and 60% of which is re-invested for basic service development for all ethnic groups adjacent to the park. However, this is not followed regularly, depriving local people of their rightful share of the income raised from tourist visits.

Upon arrival in the Mursi village, the tourist will pay 200 ETB per person ($26) as the village entrance fee to the village coordinators. Children start to dance and mothers and girls with lip cuts show off their lips, enticing tourists to take photos. Those that do not have a lip cut show off their ears with white wooden discs. Photo 3.3 shows a tourist encounter in Mursiland.

Photo 3.3: Tourist encounter in Mursiland

A photo for cash earns 5–10 ETB ($0.18–$0.36); a sale of lip plates 50ETB ($1.80); video footage, 500ETB ($18.04) to be paid to the village; and a show of bloodletting, which the Mursi drink mixed with milk, *ergehola*, earns 1000ETB ($36.08), also paid to the village. The maximum and minimum tourist earnings in one day, as recalled by 12 women, ranges between 0 and 1500ETB ($54), with an average earning of 502 ($19). The entrance fee from the tourist is divided among the households, and shares reach at times up to 5000 ETB ($180)/person per day. Tourist cash also includes sales of artifacts such as lip plates or *dhebia tugon*, ETB 50($1.80); *gorjo ye genfo* or porridge containers, ETB 600($21.65); kelle capes, up to ETB7000 ($253); and cattle decorations or *nila*, up to ETB 9000($325).

In most cases, the Mursi feel they deserve more than they get for the photo, but on the other hand, they accept what they are given because they know it is better than nothing. Some members have clearly reflected their anger and resentment at the demeaning nature of photo and cash exchange and are not interested in taking money from tourists. These are very few in number, but they understand why the majority are engaged in the activity. When some tourists refrain from taking photos, the Mursi are confused and disappointed and ask why they are there and do not take photos.

Tourist encounters last between an hour and an hour and a half. Prior to the tourist arrival, all household members prepare to meet the tourists with painted faces and bodies, and different types of objects as head adornment. Normally, the Mursi do not put objects on their bodies as adornments except for their lip plates and bracelets made of brass *lalang* for women. However, when women were asked why they put on the objects, T.T. answered: "…this is just to attract tourists; some tourists have asked us to put these objects on when they take pictures."

At one point during a conversation with a group of women, the researchers told them of the opinion tourists hold of their tribe, i.e., the perception that the Mursi wear all the adornments and heavy costumes along with jewelry as part of their culture. The revelation resulted in their surprise and added to their worries. They were all surprised to know about the perception, as they wore those adornments only to attract tourists. An elderly woman, B.O., said, "but we always thought that the tourists like for us to put stuff on ourselves. We do it for them. Those who come to take pictures ask us to wear many things and adorn ourselves heavily. This is why we do it." She then said, "I think from now on, I will not put any stuff on myself, even if they do not like it. This is not our culture." This was our discussion in early August. On the next visit in February 2019, the researcher was told that the Mursi had changed their system of taking money for a photo. They will not demand that tourists to take their photos and run after them. Instead, they will stay put and continue to do their daily chores. However, tourists will be asked to pay an extra 200 ETB ($7.21) each to take photos without limit. This system, they told me, was put in place after a big meeting among the Mursi in the tourist visiting areas to change their system. This new system was agreed upon by everyone at the time.

In August 2019, my discussion with the women in another village revealed that the system has changed there too, but the women were not sure if it was the right way to collect money. They said the money does come to the women, but the men would like to share it, as the amount is paid during entry to the coordinators.

The new system is appreciated by the tour operators and guides in Jinka, saying that it makes life easy for them, instead of mediating between tourists and local people in the exchange of photos for cash.

3.4.3   Cattle settlements: tui

A cattle settlement or *tui* is a homestead where the cattle stay for the night. The Mursi live there collectively in the months of August and September after their return from their rain-fed cultivation. Two cattle settlements served as the base for this research. The first cattle settlement is located 20 minutes to the south of the main access road (Figure 3.3). It consists of five related households that herd their cattle together. A household here means a hut with a mother and her children. My host has eight children (Household 1; Figure 3.3), six girls and two boys, as well as her stepson; Household 2 consists of a co-wife with her two children; Household 3, my host's brother and his wife with two of their children; Household 4, the husband's uncle and wife with two children, as well as an aunt and her two children; and Household 5, my host's second daughter with her husband and a child. They all move to the J tourist site and join other groups.

The second cattle settlement is located some 30 minutes away west of the main access road. This cattle settlement consists of nine households; see genealogy (Figure 3.3). My host lives in her late father's hut in Household 1, with her two children and her late father's young wife, now her older brother's third wife, with her four children and their newborn baby; her older brother living with his first wife and two children in Household 2; his second wife with their first child in Household 3; her younger brother with his bride and newborn child in Household 4; their younger sister lives nearby with her husband and their child in Household 5; their sister's father-in-law with his three wives and their children in Households 6, 7 and 8; and my host's cousin with his wife and two of their children in Household 9. The K tourist site consists of 20 huts of households that come from the nearby cattle settlements, among which K cattle settlement is one.

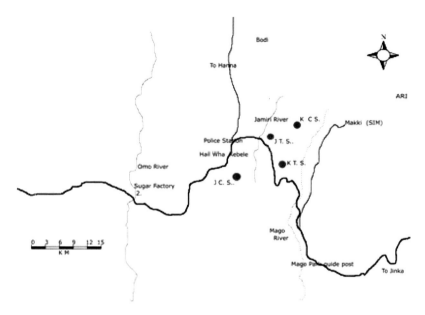

Figure 3.1: Map of the J & K cattle settlement research sites and tourist sites

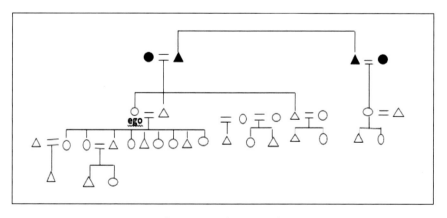

Source: Author's Work

Figure 3.2: J. Cattle settlement genealogy

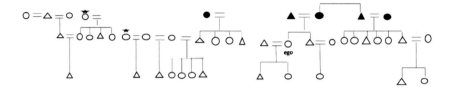

Figure 3.3: K. cattle settlement genealogy

3.4.3.1   *Preparing for tourists*

Every day the household members of the two cattle settlements, J and K, perform the daily chores of milking the cattle and providing their children breakfast. Once the daily chores are done, all members of the settlement except for the sick and the new mothers move to the tourist site (Table 3.1).

The young boys responsible for herding the cattle sometimes join the encounter, or they make their own shows on the roadside.

3.4.3.2   *Livelihood movements and tourist encounters*

After the *loru* harvest in February, the Mursi move back to their rain-fed cultivation area in March. In their rain-fed cultivation season, *telagai,* they are closer to their cattle settlements, 1 to 2 hours away. The Mursi boys/men pass through a number of age grades during the course of their lives (Turton, 1978). Children from birth until their teenage years belong to the age-grades of *dhongai* and *changalay*, at which time their role is to herd; then they move to the *teru* grade until they marry. At this age grade they live together in cattle camps, take care of their animals, and court unmarried girls (Regi, 2014). Once married, they enter the *rora* group, which is then like the police, ensuring people's safety and the herds and smooth running of internal community relations. The *bara* (junior elders) are the ones that make collective decisions for the community, and finally there are the *karui* (senior elders).

The young boys during *changalay* remain close to the cattle settlements to look after the cattle within the Elma Valley. As Turton (1986) described, the wooded grasslands at the Omo-Mago watershed, which are free from the tsetse fly and where water is available during the dry seasons, is the place where the cattle will stay during the dry season.

The *teru* and the *rora* age-grades move around when necessary to support the groups, especially during the clearing of the rain-fed cultivation. Starting from June after the harvest, all the family move to the cattle settlement and enjoy their produce and fresh milk until the next season.

The months from July to November are the tourist seasons. From July to September, the Mursi women are in their cattle settlements close to the tourist sites, combining their harvest and tourist encounters (Figure 3.4). Figure 3.5 shows women's movement during the year to balance livelihood activities. Women, being the cultivators, move constantly following the season to the different cultivation sites. The guides say that they have to remind them to leave people at the tourist sites. As their harvest does not last beyond two months, the next harvest is in January–February, and it is important to earn money from tourists to bridge the gap. Figure 3.5 shows the movement of Mursi women between their cultivation and their tourist site.

Those from distant villages also make trips to earn cash from the photos and take advantage of tourism income. Regi (2014) attests that the Mursi have changed their migration routes, which now cut across all of the territorial sections and "traditional" migration routes within the sections so as to acquire income from tourism, which he describes as the "new source of wealth."

Age range	J. Cattle Settlement		K Cattle Settlement	
	5 Households		9 Households	
	August 2017		August 2018	
	F	M	F	M
>30	4	3	5	
19-29	3	1	6	4
15 – 18	1		1	
15<	6	7	5	6
Total	14	11	17	10

Table 3.1: Daily household members move to the tourist site

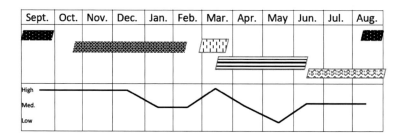

Sept.	Oct.	Nov.	Dec.	Jan.	Feb.	Mar.	Apr.	May	Jun.	Jul.	Aug.

🔲 *Lour*: Small rains

🔲 *Su*: hot season: Flood-retreat cultivation - harvest season

🔲 Issabhai (seventh month): Big rain: preparation for rain-fed cultivation

🔲 *Oiyoi:* rain-fed cultivation season

🔲 *Telagai*: collection of harvest season

— Tourist visit trend

Figure 3.4: Seasonal calendar and tourist trend in Mursiland

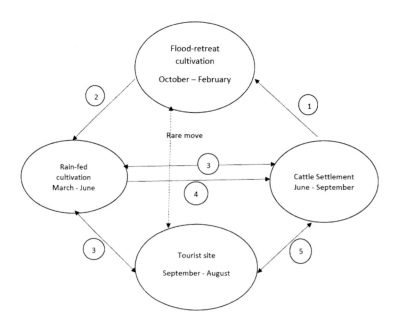

Figure 3.5: Mursi women's movement between cultivation and tourist sites

3.4.3.3   *Tourist sites (orr touristi) and tourist homes*

The tourist sites, *orr touristi*, are located by the roadside away from the cattle settlement to make them accessible by tourists. Officially, nine tourist sites were registered by the zonal office as of 2019, but some may be built seasonally and abandoned every year. Each wife builds her hut in the *orr touristi*. The huts' setup is similar to the Mursi cattle settlement, with belongings carried back and forth as they move. This is because the Mursi live a simple life that enables them to move around easily from one set of villages to another, perhaps contrary to what MacCannell (1973, 1999) described as the front stage and back stage regions of tourist settings, where the front stage regions are the social meeting spaces for outsiders, while the back stage places are for the members of the home team to retire and rest. Photo 3.4 shows a tourist encounter in the K tourist site.

However, the setup of the "Photo for Cash" scenario limits tourists from experiencing and learning about the Mursi people's diverse culture beyond what they normally are set to see. Their one and a half hours are spent only in taking pictures of the people, but very rarely do they try to learn of their way of life, cultural practices, or surroundings. This is mainly because of the tales told in the area of their violent behavior, making them seem dangerous and vicious. This nowadays is understood by the Mursi people and is a matter of regret. They say that this is why the number of tourists coming to visit has been decreasing, and they explain how their culture is respectful of guests coming to visit them, contrary to what is told about them. This in fact is demonstrated whenever there is any conflict in the area; cars with tourists are always safe to move around.

Once women arrive at the site, they continue their daily chores until the tourists arrive. Grinding grain for the daily meal of *tila*, preparing *gesso*, the local grain-based drink, for sale, looking after their children, and collecting firewood, water, and gathering leaves from the nearby bush to prepare *kinui* an accompaniment for *tila* continue as the daily chores.

The majority of the Mursi (75%) are from the Dola groups (Turton, 1995), and the tourist encounter sites are within the territory in the northern part, where the access road intersects. Those coming from further away from the access road, the Ariholi and Gongulobibi, travel into the tourist sites on a daily basis to meet the tourists. The sites are mostly coordinated by men. The men in Mursi pass through functional age groups during the course of their lives. The senior elders (*bari*) often observe the day's happenings during tourist visits from afar. The *teru* and the *rora* collectively coordinating the contact and link between the people, the guides, and the tourist. In the K tourist site, one of the three coordinators is a woman, who is well connected with the city of Jinka and also has links with some tourists.

3.4.3.4   *Tourist reflections on the tourist scenario in Mursi at the tourist site*

The typology of tourists in Mursi can be identified as incipient mass tourists, categorized by Smith (1989) as those with a steady flow and those who are not comfortable participating or closely interacting with the local people. They seek western-style amenities and demand comfort. Likewise, the tourists coming to Mursi are not willing to stay any longer than an hour.

They will quickly take pictures and want to go back to the city to transfer to their next site. It is very rare for tourists to ask to stay and camp in the forested area. The Mursi are puzzled why they are quick to go back and do not want to stay longer.

A quick conversation with tourists visiting the tourist site reflects their worry about taking photos or not and whether to give money. They mostly worry, following what they have been told, that the money they give will be used for buying drinks. A French tourist asked, "Will the women get part of the money that is given at the village? Is it okay for me to give money for the photo? If I do, will the women get it?" Mostly tourists coming from Europe are conscious of such aspects of their dealings with the local people. Some of them refrain from taking photos. These disturb local people and ask, "Why do they come to visit and not take pictures?"

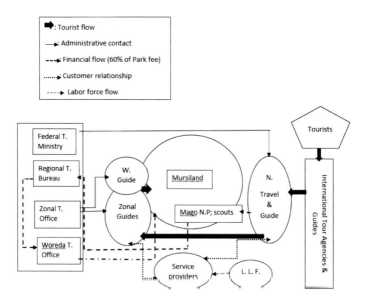

Figure 3.6: Schematic of stakeholders and tourist flow in Mursiland

3.4.4   *Stakeholders in the Mursi tourism scenario*

The Mursi tourism scenario involves many stakeholders in bringing the tourists for encounters with the local people, as illustrated in the schematics below (Figure 3.6). Here I outline the main stakeholders.

3.4.4.1   *Local people*

These are the Mursi living in the vicinity of the tourist sites and those who come from afar to encounter tourists on a daily basis. As indicated above, the local people are organized to receive the tourists and guides every day. Local people often complain that the guides act like gatekeepers and intercept money that tourists are willing to give them. Still, because they know they are the only means of receiving tourist visits, they remain silent and receive whatever they are shared. This is a power relation that disturbs the Mursi, but they are helpless to fix the situation. Lately, they have managed to communicate with the local authorities in case the guides do not visit their sites as expected. Officially, this is the first contact with the local authority within this year, as they do not have any formal contact with the local authorities and they are not in any way within the tourism sector structure. It is just recognized that tourists come and visit these tourist sites, but local authorities never make any visit or check any of the tourist destinations.

3.4.4.2   *Local guide association members*

Local guides at the zonal level and at the woreda level coordinate their guiding services in Mursi on a rotational basis. In the zone, all guides operate only with woreda guides. Each woreda has its own guide association. Normally, the zonal guides who were the first to set up an association within the zone have the liberty to go into all the woredas and work and share with the woreda local guides. When it comes to Mursiland, the zonal and woreda guides have made arrangements to work together and work on a three-day rotational basis. Guiding services are a major job opportunity for the youth in SOZ. The local authorities recognize this; therefore, they encourage more young people to be absorbed into the existing groups. This sometimes creates conflicts with the old and seasoned guide association members. This, they say, reduces the quality of the service as well as their revenue.

3.4.4.3   *Local travel and tour organizations*

These are tourist organizations that normally work at the national level based in Addis Ababa. Mostly they work with the zonal guides and make arrangements for the visit to sites. They make contact directly with woreda guides based on existing contacts. The travel and tour companies are all local, but they are not involved in direct contact with the local people at the destination. In fact, no tour companies can reach any of the tourist's sites without the knowledge of the guides. This mainly serves to maintain the benefits of the local guide associations from the tourist payments, and is therefore observed by all travel agencies coming to the site.

3.4.4.4   *Local authorities*

The local authorities directly contact the guides at the zonal and woreda levels and service providers like hotels and restaurants. Their main role is to regulate the guides, provide training, and demand monthly reports of tourist visits. Until recently, the Mursi did not have any direct link with the local authority; however, lately the Mursi have been said to be making direct contact with the local authority and are making demands of tourist visits through the guides to be regulated by the local authority. As a result, a letter has been written to all guide association to insist that they visit all sites equally and fairly (Annex Letter IV) to give an equal chance to all tourist sites, as guides discriminate between sites based on special connections with certain tourist sites. As a result, the Mursi have demanded that the zonal office officially direct guides to take tourists to all sites. The zonal office said they had written a list of the tourist sites to be visited and the local guides were instructed to follow the rules to give all the sites an equal chance.

The local authority in the zone or woreda has no direct engagement in monitoring or providing any assistance to tourist sites in the zone. The sentiment in the zone is to remain indifferent to tourism activity at destination. No direct engagement is witnessed, and the staff admit their limited knowledge of or interaction with the people at the destination who are the main attraction of tourists in the zone. The staff clearly admit that the office does not have any clear direction on how to engage with people at the destination. This clearly shows neglect on the government's side at the zonal level, but it is clearly linked to the sectoral tourism policy at all levels, leaving local people at the destination powerless.

3.5   Livelihood assets in Mursiland

During the FGD exercise in Mursiland, 12 participants attended two half-days at the South Omo Research Center to undertake asset mapping, self-evaluation, and identification of wellbeing indicators (Photo 3.4). Participants came from three villages, the K, J, and M cattle settlements. M. village is a cattle settlement that does not receive tourists today, although initially it was the first site that received tourists, according to local peoples' recollection.

Photo 3.4: FGD session at South Omo Research Center (SORC)

3.5.1   Natural capital

In Mursi, assets were described as '*Babaga—Shumunugnet*' during the participants' focus group discussion. In Mursi the rivers (*kido*) Omo ma *warr, elma,* and *makki/mako* are the main means for their flood retreat cultivation, where they produce grain such as sorghum, *liwa*; find fruit, *komkare*; fish, *arguli*; obtain roots, *keno kirema*; set up beehives, *guidoy*; and also find different types of wild animals like hippos. It is also a place of recreation, *sani*, swimming *zami*, and watering their cattle, and where women collect a type of clay, edir and tsdy, to make earrings and lip plates, *dhebi a tugon.* The grassland is for grazing their animals and the forest, *gashi,* for their rain-fed cultivation, *gugna,* for collecting honey, *retey,* and to collect different kinds of medicinal plants like African wild olive, *girari*.

3.5.2   Financial capital

For Mursi, cash is normally raised by selling their cattle. However, livestock are not sold just to make money but for a specific occasion and purpose. To pastoralists, livestock is very valuable beyond its function as a source of food and insurance. Their social function, as the gift for a bride-wealth, makes them highly valued. As a result, the Mursi are very reluctant to sell their cattle. Today, cash earned from tourism is identified as an alternative means to raise cash and therefore maintain their valuable asset, their livestock. A kind of risk management also applies of building up their assets for resilience in harsh times.

3.5.3   Physical capital

The Mursi identified the road as one important asset they value, as it is a means for tourists to visit and for the ambulance to reach them during an emergency to take them to the nearest health post or hospital in Jinka.

The schools in Makki (not near all Mursi, as it is in the northern part) were also indicated as valuable assets for students. The girls and boys of one Kebelle, Makki, attend school at the missionary center of the Sudanese Interior Mission (SIM), which is close to the Kebelle. Two elementary schools are available, providing schooling to the nearby Mursi community. Beyond the elementary schools, students go to Jinak, Hawassa, or Arbaminch, the nearest cities within the region. In Jinka, the government runs hostels for all the agro-pastoralist students to encourage them to continue their school beyond the elementary level. All facilities are paid for by the zonal government until they finish high school. The facilities, however, are not consistent, as students often complain about the services provided. In October 2019, students complained that the facility was not set up for the whole month in October, and students had already started their school but had no food or other necessary services required in a boarding hostel. Complaint to the zonal office only resulted in a request that they wait and use their own means until the office could finalize the transfer of funds.

The group recognized education as a means to enable groups to gain the upper hand in accessing tourist activity. Villages with educated members are said to have a better connection with guides, and even connect directly with tourists using computers and emails; also, they recognize that these groups have a better connection with the local authority and the possibility of engaging in local politics at the woreda and zonal level. This assured better access to the tourism business. Photo 3.6 shows local Mursi men discussing assets in Mursiland and working on a digital paper during the focus group discussion exercise.

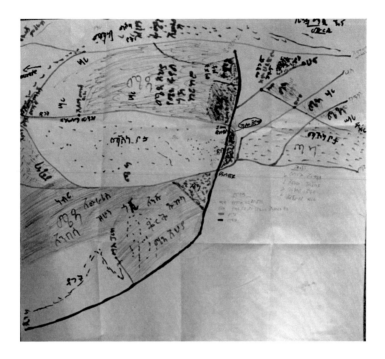

Photo 3.5: Map of Mursiland

3.5.4   *Human capital*

Not raised during the FGD but based on my observation, the Mursi highly depend on their local knowledge and skills to survive, although in their discussions they indicated the importance of education today, particularly raising the issue of how tourist sites with educated members receive more tourists; they thus believe that they have to educate themselves. Yet, children do not have facilities nearby to go to school. In both of the research villages, all young boys and girls do not go to school. Still, the children have all their daily routines mixed with their time of play and tasks. Young girls will still help collect firewood and water from the nearby river for the family, helping their mothers in milling starting from an early age, roughly 10 years. Young boys in *dhongai*, around the age of 11–12, will start looking after their cattle. This age will be their start in the Mursi age grade, a journey towards their age set.

Health facilities also not accessible unless they travel to the nearest towns of Hanna or Jinka. However, they said their health security is always dependent on natural remedies with plants through local healers. Their livestock is their main source for healing. During a health crisis, a family will kill a cow to drink the soup. This they say is their major source of healing and health. During my interview in J village, women said that for them, their livestock is their life, "…the Mun if they have their livestock, everything else is secondary."

Photo 3.6: Resource mapping – men's FGD in K. tourist site

3.5.5   *Social capital*

The Mursi people have high regard for their social networks. Although not explicitly raised during the FGD as a category and asset, this was highlighted during the discussion and interview. In a discussion with a prominent Mursi elder who is well connected nationally and internationally, M.S. said, "the Mursi are 'one'; we all look out for each other. This is the only way to survive. If one is hungry, everybody is hungry; if one is attacked, everyone is attacked."

Although a specific group will set up a tourist sites, there is no limitation for anyone from near or far villages to encounter tourists and earn cash. Often when a tourist is reported to arrive through a call from a guide in town all will start from their cattle settlements earlier than normal. After they arrive, more people will also arrive from remote villages to meet the tourists.

Mobile phones have become quite valuable for the Mursi to instantly pass information among themselves and their networks in town, such as connections with the guides in Jinka. This connection also creates a means to access the market in Jinka, where guides assist in purchasing grain, flour, and other necessary items and send it to the villages through public transport or bring it themselves on their next trip to the village.

During an FGD exercise for women in J and K cattle settlements, when asked what their best times are, they stated, "for us, receiving our guests, having enough grain to feed our guests…with a demonstration of grinding more and more…and providing the guests with food and drink is a good time," and "the singing and dancing in preparation for a wedding, going to our son's favored girl's area to see her and sing and dance, and the girls and women's fight with their iron bracelet *ula* is the most enjoyable." This fight is described by LaTosky (2010) as the *ula* competition, a kind of "male audience" show performed by girls showing off their strong strokes, which demonstrate their strength and thus suitability for marriage.

3.6   Assets and drivers of livelihood strategy in cultural tourism in Mursiland

3.6.1   Cultural capital/assets as a basis for a livelihood strategy

The evidence in this research demonstrates that their cultural assets create opportunities for an alternative livelihood for local people in Mursi, in this case, their unique identity, tradition, and value systems. This opportunity is mainly for girls and women, as tourists' primary interest is to visit women and girls with lip cuts and lip plates. However, tourists in Mursi visit the whole village, and men and young boys also have opportunities to earn cash. This means that Mursi, who are dependent on only their livestock for cash, find cultural tourism to provide significant access to extra cash and to diversify their livelihood.

3.6.2   Social relations determining access to livelihood opportunities

In Mursi, the opportunity of a tourist encounter is determined by the coordinators' networking ability with guide association members. Mobile phones play an important role. This connection also assists in mobilizing the purchase of grain and flour in Jinka. Cash earned from tourists is given to guides, and selected guides facilitate the purchase and transport of grain and flour to Mursiland. Still, good networking and knowing the right kind of guide always increase the visits of tourists to each of the tourist sites.

3.6.3   *Vulnerability as drivers for livelihood strategies*

The livelihood in Mursiland is recurrently precarious. External shocks such as variability in rainfall, slow-onset drought, and pest infestation are everyday challenges that put the Mursi in a vulnerable position.

An interview with the early warning department head at SOZ in Jinka reveals that Salamago woreda, where Mursi is located, is normally not considered food insecure because of the cattle and the good amounts of grazing land. In their rapid assessment of food insecurity, their indicator for the Mursi is their grazing land quality. Their assumption is that if their livestock is in good condition, so are the people. In such cases they will have milk, and under the worst conditions, they can sell cattle to purchase grain, leaving them more prepared than other neighboring groups. In 2017, however, as per an interview with the zonal officer, there was a shortage recorded where some 14,000 people needed support within the woreda because of a fall armyworm infestation and drought due to the failure of the big rain in March. In 2018 the number was reduced to 8,319, but due to ongoing drought from failed big rain, there was a reduction of the harvest of 20%–35% from the previous year. Normally, support from the zonal office to the woreda is more concerned with short-term stress than permanent support for food security assistance programs.

Contrary to the local authority's description, the Mursi's assessment of their own situation is often dire, with complaints of recurrent hunger and the constant need for extra grain, which lacks government support.

The Mursi describe their consistent hunger due to the shortage of grain. In 2017 in J village, fresh milk was available for the children and some buttermilk for adults to accompany their *tilla*. Still, my host complained of a grain shortage for the family. In 2018, even children did not have fresh milk to drink in K village, and they reported a grain shortage for the family. The number of meals was limited to a maximum of twice a day, but the norm was once a day.

Livestock selling during vulnerable times is one major strategy in Mursi. However, sale of livestock is not very easy. Cattle sold in Jinka have a very high transportation cost to Mursi. They will have to be paid a good amount to walk the cattle 70km to get to Jinka. Tefera et al. (2012) stressed that poor access to livestock markets because of bad access roads leads to high transportation costs. So, usually, bartering cattle for grain is the normal system, which is only sold in times of hardship.

3.6.3.1   *Coping strategies*

Coping is a short-term response to an unexpected crisis (Davis, 1996). Observation in Mursi revealed that in times of grain shortage o after a bad harvest, local people increase the collection of wild fruits, leaves, and roots from the nearby bushes as a coping strategy (Photo 3.7); nearly 50 types of leaves, fruits, and roots were identified that can be collected and consumed. Moreover, hunting for wild animals in the forest, usually warthogs, or *hoy*; sharing food, as in Mursi people share their daily meal with friends and family; and planting Mursi maize, a drought-resistant type, and early maturing grain have been indicated as their means of coping during difficult times. Local people also report that tourist cash assists in their coping strategies.

Women make *gesso* (a grain-based drink) from the bad grain after a bad harvest due to pests or failed rain for consumption or for sale to raise cash to purchase good grain. In 2018, two women in the K tourist site sold *gesso* worth 1000 ETB ($34), and another woman sold *gesso* worth 4,000 ($144) and sent to Jinka to buy grain/flour. They said a 100kg bag of grain could make *gesso* that would sell for up to 10,000 ETB ($148), and cash worth $14–$18 can buy 100kg of maize.

Three senior elders, sitting and observing the tourist encounter in K *orr touristi* in 2018 responded to a question about why tourist money is important:

> *Elder: Tourisi chahlii (tourists are good)* ...
> *Me: Why?*
> *Elder: Tourist brings money.*
> *Me: Money for what?*
> *Elder: To buy maize (kona) and sorghum (doli).*
> *Me: But you have your own cultivated grain?*
> *Elder: Too much rain destroyed our grain, the rain is not good, sometimes too much and sometimes too little.*

One of the heads of a household in village M, not accessible to tourists, complained of their shortage of grain even in August 2018, right after the harvest season, and their worry, as their only resort is to sell cattle, an option they wished to avoid. Figure 3.7 shows the bimodal season in Mursiland from the average monthly records of 10 years of rainfall and temperature.

The Mursi report that cash from tourism plays a major role during harsh times resulting from crop failure. During fieldwork in 2018, I witnessed members of the

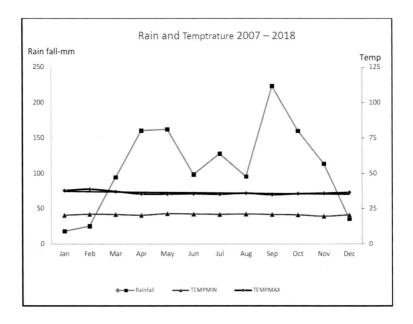

Figure 3.7: Rain and Temperature in Hanna, Salamago, 2007–2018

Photo 3.7: Fruits and greens from the forest (October 2018)

K tourist site sending a total of 4,000 ETB ($144) cash from the village fee received from tourists through a guide to purchase grain/flour from Jinka. In this case, tourist cash enables the purchase of grain to manage consumption in the short term as a response to an external shock such as rain variability leading to drought and pests that affect their production.

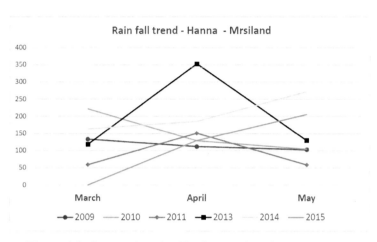

Figure 3.8: Seasonal variability in the big rain, March–May

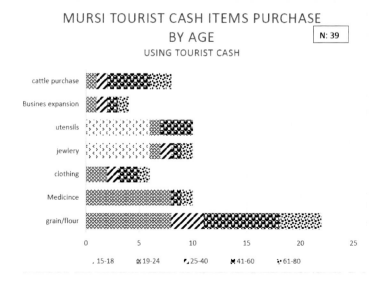

Figure 3.9: Mursi tourist cash item purchases by age

3.6.3.2   *Risk management in the long term*

Tourist cash also provides an opportunity to build their capability to resist shocks in the long term by building their assets, changing their asset mix, and diversifying their income sources, which can be termed an adaptation strategy (Davis, 1996; Ellis, 2000; Opiyo et al., 2015). This is now a contemporary practice among the Mursi people in the tourist sites. This is one major reason why the Mursi people at tourist destinations are interested in pursuing tourist cash. During better times, i.e., when they have a good harvest, money from selling crops is used to purchase cattle or goats.

Interviews with 39 individuals at both tourist sites during tourist encounters revealed that 22 of the Mursi interviewed use cash earned from tourists to purchase grain/flour (Figure 3.9), and 10 used it to cover medical fees; these are in the age groups 19–80. Young Mursi in the age range 15–18 usually use their cash for jewelry and some to buy utensils, probably in preparation for marriage. Age groups over 41 years of age spend their cash on purchasing cattle, and secondarily grain/flour.

3.7   Access to and control over cash for women

Tourist cash also provides the means to finance women's small businesses, such as purchasing ingredients for *gesso* (grain-based drink) or purchasing *areke* (grain-based liquor) from town to sell in Mursi, as well as grain and flour to be sold to far-off villages.

Tourist cash in Mursi has created the opportunity for women to earn and control cash. This means that women can use the cash they earn from tourists independently. Women say tourist cash is essential for their medical needs and for starting or expanding their businesses, purchasing flour to avoid grinding grain, and saving to purchase cattle or goats (see Figure 4). One mother revealed that with savings of 10,000ETB ($148) from tourist cash, she managed to buy four calves, three of which contributed to her son's bride-wealth.

A women-only focus group discussion in J cattle settlement described their means of living:

> *Cattle are our life. If children are sick, we make soup, and we do not have to go to the hospital. These days there is this clinic, maybe it is better, but we have to pay for the clinic…*

3.7.1   *Girls' lip cutting and tourist cash*

In recent years, Mursi girls have maintained their long-held lip cutting practice, thereby hugely altering the tourism dynamics in Mursiland. Lip cutting can be taken as a marker (Elder et al., 2003) according to the social pathway or cultural script theory. This is because lip cutting in Mursi girls is a way of transitioning into adulthood (LaTosky, 2009; Turton, 2004) that also signifies sexual maturity and beauty. In the past, a Mursi girl without a lip cut and plate was considered a *ngidi* or Kwegu, a neighboring ethnic group that the Mursi consider inferior (Turton, 1986), and thus indicating a position not appreciated in Mursi; therefore, it is a marker of identity as well. Associated with this identity, the Mursi cut lips and plate have become the most lucrative tourist attraction in the zone; therefore, it has also created wealth and economic betterment (Regi, 2014).

Girls are aware of this feature lip cutting, which is the main factor in attracting tourists and thus is important to their unique identity and its economic benefit. However, recent trends show that the number of girls with lip cuts is decreasing.

One girl, asked why she no longer has her lip cut, said, "I don't cut my lips because it hurts," and when asked about the culture that requires girls to have their lips cut replied, " what does culture do?" ጎፍ ᎋ ኣኅ. For a society rooted in its culture and organized by internal social norms, it was surprising to get such a response. Still, the girls have the support of their community, as all clearly say that the girls' decision is their own. An interview with three generations of women, a grandmother, T.B., 80 years old, living with her daughter T.M., 60 years old—both with lips cut—and a granddaughter of 19 years with a one-year-old daughter, and who is not lip cut, discussed the current lip cutting scenario (Photo 3.8). To the question whether girls are abandoning lip cutting and what they think about it, T.B said, "Tourists want lip cut women, but young girls do not want to cut their lips today, but that is ok too." T.B.'s grandson B.N, who was listening to the conversation and who has a wife with no lip cut said, "We are happy with our girls without the lip plates…"

In an observation of 95 female respondents of mixed age groups, 65% of the girls and women were without lip cuts. This trend is probably in response to a long-term government campaign to abolish harmful traditional practices that started in 1978 during the Derg regime (LaTosky, 2013). This trend has continued since the advent of the EPRDF (see Fig. 3.10), and evidence shows a slowly changing trend of lip cut girls that turned entirely after 2000. Today, most young girls have uncut lips and are not interested in having their lips cut.

Photo 3.8: Interview with three generation of women in Mursiland: Lip cutting

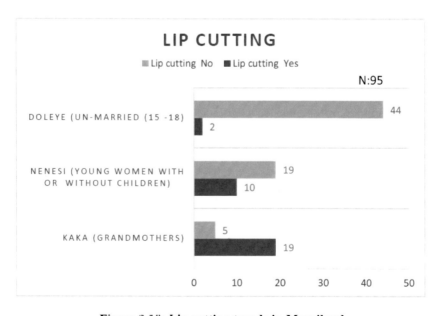

Figure 3.10: Lip cutting trends in Mursiland

3.7.1.1   Girls' education and lip cutting

According to observations, young girls, whether educated or not, are abandoning lip cutting. All interviewed girls not going to school strongly believe that they do not need to cut their lips. The majority of the girls in Mursi do not go to school. Still, all agree that they do not need to have their lips cut, as it hurts and they wish to avoid the pain. This is openly said, and they are under no pressure from their community for abandoning what is their primary identity in the zone and in particular a source of income today that has also been reported to be a means of coping. Table 3.2 shows an interview with 26 women and girls showing the educational level of participants in relation to lip cutting.

3.7.1.2   Effect of lip cutting trends on Mursi livelihood

The new trend is having an effect on the Mursi people engaged in tourism pursuit for livelihood through cultural tourism. Guides today make the choice to take tourists to places where most of the girls and women have lip cuts. As a result, old tourist sites lose out on tourist visits because most girls have abandoned their lip cuts. When asked what happens with the tourists, girls with no lip cuts replied that they put on their adornments and wooden ear plates to entice tourists to take their photo. This is borne out by observation. Girls are very proud, showing off their huge ear wooden plates, and still earn tourist cash. Their decision not to cut their lips even though it is expected of them demonstrates the girls' agency (Hitlin et.al., 2006; Hitlin and Elder, 2007) all the more so as tourist money is important for them by providing a unique financial advantage to cover their particular needs, such as jewelry. It also has an important advantage in allowing them to own a mobile phone, which is becoming very popular among young girls in Mursi, as it requires a regular cash flow to maintain the connection. As LaToysk (2010) said, tourist cash is a way of wealth building for young girls and boys today. Still, all these girls stand strong on abandoning their lip cutting while continuing with their tourist encounters on their own terms and defining their new identity themselves.

Table 3.2: Girls' education and lip cutting

Education vs lip cut   N. 26

	schooled	non schooled
Lip cut	0	8
No lip cut	4	12

3.8   The life story of a Mursi mother: The story of G.W.

G.W. was my host, and we have had conversations about her life on several occasions. The purpose was to gain insight into the pattern of her life, so as to understand more people's lives in Mursiland and their relationship with cultural tourism.

G.W. described her life as having turmoil from the beginning. She was born in a time of war between the Hamer and the Mursi, followed by a cholera epidemic that killed many of the children, but she survived. She said it was a local medicine that stopped the ailment.

She grew up and married. When her first child was born, another war started between the Mursi and the Nyangatom ethnic group, then famine followed. At that time, people started to migrate to other places: Menit, Ari, Maki, and Balmir. She said her life is filled with memories of all those bad times. She said, "the good times are our cultural tradition during wedding ceremonies of the songs and dance, traditional girls` fight with their iron bracelets, *ula*, similar to the stick dueling *donga* for men, where the fun is supporting our team. Our main challenge is war and disease".

"For our livelihood." she said, "we live in the forest, we get everything we need here, grass for our cattle, we clear the forest to cultivate sorghum *dali*, we can have red or white sorghum, and also cultivate maize *kono*. If we cannot produce enough, we have to move to other places. Moving is tough, but it is our life and we do it. The dry season is the harshest time for women. The sun is too dry and scorching. When the sun is too hot, water fetching becomes tiring, as it is difficult to find water nearby, and our cattle do not have enough to graze or drink."

"To cultivate is the mother's role. Prepare the land, sow, and protect crop from birds and monkeys. As a result, we have to stay there until harvest. Once it is dry, we thresh it with a stick and collect it to put in our storage. Men and boys will herd the cattle. After harvest, all the grain is collected, and the wedding season starts. The dance and fights. It is a good time and merry time after a good harvest, it is when girls and boys notice each other for love. At times girls get abducted, get pregnant, but then she comes back to her family, then the family gets together, and wise *shimaglewoch* drink coffee and make up."

"For food we eat what is at home. Sorghum and maize the women and girls mill to make porridge *tila* to eat with fresh milk *urachaga*, and buttermilk *kirana*. We also prepare accompaniment with cooked wild leaves *kinui*, if available with meat. The boys can have milk and blood *ergehola*." Showing her hands, she says, "our hands get tough and sore from milling the sorghum or maize to make porridge, look at mine and N's," comparing it to the hands of her daughter, who was a 10th-grade student in 2017 in the nearby town of Jinka. She "this life is difficult for me". In 2018 she got married and returned back to Mursiland.

3.8.1   *Lip plates and tourists*

"In my time, Mursi women would have a lip cut and a lip plate made of clay, a *dhebia tugony*. It is an adornment for the woman but she also has an obligation to wear it when she serves food and water to her husband. In case she does not comply, then she will be flogged. My daughter does not have to do that now. If she wants it as an ornament, she can have it, but there is no obligation."

"Tourists like it, so we put it on for them. The tourist comes to visit, and they give us 5–10 ETB ($0.18–$0.36) for each photo. This we use to buy grain from Jinka, get it milled, and bring it to consume. Most men use their money to buy drink, *areke* (a grain-based liquor produced in Jinka). They buy two liters in Jinka for 100 ETB ($1.40), and sell it for 200 ETB ($2.81) in Mursiland."

G.W. recollected a tourist encounter about 18 years ago. She recalls that there were difficulties—drought and famine; people were hungry and there was no rain. The government was giving food ration at a place called Dildilli. Livestock were sick with an illness (*gomai*) that the Mursi thought was witchcraft. The livestock in the Makki area (in the north of Mursi) were badly hit.

At the time, G.W. recalls, there were two *kumarus*, a kind of a priest for the Mursi. There was one in the south and one in the north; the one in the south, she said, was not a good one.

She said, "At the time the tourists came and pay 50 ETB per person (village entrance) and paid us only 1 ETB ($0.01). Today, the village fee is $200, and when the number of tourists is good, we can get up to 500 ETB ($7.04) per day, otherwise on a normal day we get 100 ETB ($1.40) from photos." In the past five years (interview in 2017), "we have not gone to the forest to cultivate. The money we get from tourists is good, so we can buy grain. However, the guides usually take part of what we earn. If not for them, we could have saved more. These days, the rain is too heavy and destroys our harvest, so with the tourist money at least we survive."

She said, ".... The tourist money is good, but our cattle are important.... anyone who does not have cattle is .... like you when you have no education. He cannot do anything. If we are sick, that is what we have ...we make soup of the meat, and we get healed, if we want to go to the clinic in Jinka, then we need cash."

Recently, in 2018, a new system was set up for receiving money from tourists. Now tourists were made to pay an extra 200 ETB ($2.81) per person for photo taking. This was organized after a large meeting in August 2018 on how to meet tourists. Since then, G.W. said, "We were told when the tourist come, to just stay still and continue to do our jobs. The tourist can come and take pictures as they want, as they have been asked to pay in the beginning." The money is later shared among all the women. At the time, G.W. said, they do take the money, but the men also want to share. She said it is a relatively new system, yet the women are still discussing how to continue it.

3.8.2   *Reflections on her life story*

G.W. recollects all the harsh, trying times of war, sickness, and famine in her life. These elements come into her account several times. Their life requires moving, and if all is good, they have everything in their surroundings. The role of women cultivators is harsh in reality due the external shocks that exacerbate their livelihood, compounded with women's additional suffering due to water scarcity and the drudgery of milling that adds to their difficult gender role and makes life conditions difficult. The significance of the tourism encounters in G.W.'s life trajectory is shown by the fact that tourist cash allows them a means of coping to alleviate the harsh reality in her vulnerable livelihood. To some extent, it is also reflected in the fact that cultivation is traded off against cash earning from tourism due to its minimized risk even though the earning is inadequate based on their own valuation.

3.8.3   A day with G.W. in J cattle settlement (Wednesday, September 2017)

The morning is cool and slightly drizzly. My host, G.W., is the first to get up at around 5 am with her two-year-old girl M. I can hear them having a sweet conversation. I was watching from my tent, seeing just their frames in the dawn. All the children are sleeping near the fire from last night. Then all the other mothers start to join G.W. who started the fire. All the mothers start to go to milk the cows. Once they finish milking, they give all the little children jugs full of fresh milk to drink. I joined them, and I saw one of the teenage boys taking his milk directly from the cow's udders. N., my host's daughter, asked me to take some photos; I gave her the camera and she started taking pictures. The mothers start to churn milk to drink, and some started to make porridge. After the milking was finished, my translator, her friend who stayed with us the night, and I were given porridge and buttermilk for breakfast. It was good.

Like a daily practice, we all went to the tourist site. N. is excited about her photo taking. She was going around and taking photos. They told her to pay them 20 ETB; otherwise, she could not take the photo as a joke. After a while, one family brought fresh meat to sell. G.W. bought some and started to roast it on the open fire. I asked where the meat came from. She said a family slaughtered a caw to sell the meat. Some of the girls start to decorate their faces to prepare for the tourists. Around 9 am, tourists start to come. This time they are Australian tourists in a big group, over 10 tourists. All the mothers who were milling and cooking started to put on the objects they use to adorn themselves when the tourists take photos. It was chaos.

They all mingle around to meet the tourists and let them take pictures. The tourists went around the place and took lots of pictures. Then they asked to take a video. They were told to pay 500 ETB to take a video. They agreed and started filming. N. asked me again for the camera to take a photo of the tourist, which she did. They were surprised to see a Mursi with a camera. They jokingly said she had to pay them. She took some photos.

The tourists left after about an hour and a half. No other tourists came after them. The girls and women were now gathered, and some were milling, others were just resting under the tree. Some of them were grooming each other. Young teenagers were listening to music on their mobile phones. They take turns milling and letting those with children rest. I asked to try milling. It is hard work; I managed it but got tired quickly.

N. asked me to join her to go to the nearby river to fetch water. Other girls joined us. We walked around twenty minutes and found a kind of a micro-pond and a creek constructed for the animals. The girls started to wash up. We collected water from the little creek and returned back to the hut. G.W. was still milling. Then around 4 pm she said she would go to the cattle settlement. We stayed in the tourist site, walking around and taking pictures, and visited the neighborhood. We met a lady making *gesso*.

Around 5 pm, we went back to the cattle settlement. N. immediately started to mill to make porridge for dinner. G.W. was cooking some of the beef and vegetables. After finishing her milling, she once again went to the river with her friend to wash up. At this time, they all went to the river to wash up. G.W. was still roasting some meat. This time it was even tastier, with salt and chilis. It got very dark at 7 pm. N. made porridge, and everyone started to eat it together with the meat and some greens that G. W. prepared. It was very tasty. They explained that they use eight types of leaves that they cook to eat with their porridge; they are called *kinui*. Photo 3.9 shows a mother making *gesso*.

Photo 3.9: Gesso making in Mursi

3.9   The effects of cultural tourism on wellbeing in Mursiland

In this study, two types of wellbeing assessments were conducted to gauge the connection and effects of cultural tourism on local people's wellbeing. The first was a participatory exercise that involved local people in a FGD defining what wellbeing means to them and, based on that, to value or rate the contribution of tourism benefits. The second scored 51 local people's perception of their overall wellbeing, quality of life, or life satisfaction using a Likert-scale questionnaire.

3.9.1   Identification of participatory wellbeing indicators in Mursiland

During the FGD session, participants tried to identify indicators of wellbeing in their own terms based on their evaluation of a good life. Wellbeing was first translated into their language as *lola*, a good life. This *lola* was then described and agreed upon by the participants as being when one is endowed with a number of cattle and a number of storage areas full of grain harvested during both cultivation seasons. The participants then divided the type of life in Mursi into three categories according to the level of their quality of life.

Lukuma delleley or *danka*, all meaning a person with *lola*, is a person with 3or 4 storage huts, 30 quintals of grain, 200 cattle, 120 goats, good health and education, and a number of daughters. Daughters are said to be like ivory, highly prized because they bring wealth through bride-wealth in the form of cattle. This category also includes animals without disease.

Those in the medium category are the *kadgnogi*, hardworking to make life better, with two grain storages; 10 quintals of grain; 150 cattle, 40 goats. These are also healthy and have moderate life.

On the other side, *ropga*, a bad life, is the third category, which means hunger with no grain and milk, and animal and human diseases. The life of the poor, *peoga*, is that of the poorest of the poor: an orphan who could not marry because of lack of cattle, or a widow who does not own even working tools or utensils (*shirko*) in the house

All in these categories participate in the tourism scenario, and all have different needs and expectations combined with their main livelihood patterns. Table 3.3 shows the outcome of focus group discussion exercise.

3.9.1.1   Girls as wellbeing indicators

Among the indicators, particularly in the category of *lola*, girls are described as bringing good life. For the Mursi, to have girls means gaining more cattle.

Cattle are the most important asset, not only for food or as insurance during hard times, but as one of the most critical factors in the marriage ritual: bride-wealth, as in any pastoralist community. This, however, has been a challenging situation for girls, as the marriage arrangement is often based on the amount of cattle their family will gain, and girls are rebelling against this tradition.

The tragedy is that the girls in Mursi are not like girls in most rural areas in Ethiopia, who flee to the nearest town or city. In Mursi, young girls kill themselves to avoid marrying a person without their consent. During our FDG discussion, a young man complained that these days young girls are difficult and do not accept their families' recommendations for marriage; he was fiercely criticized by a young girl who goes to school, saying, "it is you, men who do not understand us... you care more for your cattle than us." This occurrence of suicide or a girl fleeing from one place to another happens so often that almost a day does not go by without hearing that so-and-so has fled or killed herself. The difficulty of the situation is that girls are entangled within this system of livelihood and important social values that makes it very difficult even to discuss it among the Mursi. During the women-only FGD, this issue was the first one raised. One mother, after hearing a young girl complain about the situation, admitted the difficulty for young girls. She said mothers are going through a very hard time. They do not want to give away their girls without their consent. However, fathers do not even give the mother the chance to listen, and sometimes they are beaten for complaining.

Following the asset mapping, participants were asked to compare the benefit they receive from tourists to the kind of wellbeing they have now based on their schema by rating the benefit from tourism on a scale of 0–10. The valuation of the FGD participants was 2, meaning that even though tourist money contributes to their livelihood, its level of benefit to their lives is low. Nonetheless, they said that even if it is limited, it is invaluable; every amount of extra cash they earn helps to purchase grain, which is critical for their lives.

3.10   Perception of overall wellbeing/life satisfaction of local people in Mursiland

A Likert-scale questionnaire was conducted to assess the quality of life/life satisfaction of local Mursi people at the destination. Fifty-one respondents participated in the survey to answer questions divided into four wellbeing domains: Material, Community, Emotional, and Health and Safety wellbeing. The response scale had five options: *highly dissatisfied* (1), *not satisfied* (2), *moderate* (3), *satisfied* (4), and *highly satisfied* (5). The result, presented in Figure 3.11, shows that the average mean score of the QOL is 4 (*SD* = 0.57).

This can be interpreted as indicating that the overall quality of life/wellbeing perception of Mursi people at the destination is "satisfied." The local people still think there is room for improvement. During the qualitative interviews they expressed the view that tourist visits are determined by the quality of their relationship with the guides, and that to some extent the cash earned is not substantial enough to make a huge difference.

However, in Mursi, the modality of the tourist payment is very clear, and it is adhered to by the guides, so once tourists are on site, obtaining their money is secured. None of the guides can attempt to withhold payment or say they will be paid the next time. All tourists have to pay the village entrance fee upon entry to the village, and only then can they make contact with the rest of the group. This may be the reason that it is perceived as satisfactory.

Considering each domain of the QOL in terms of the Likert-scored questions affords us a detailed view of how the local people at the destination responded. These results are also compared to the Likert scores for the economic, social, cultural, and environmental impacts of tourism.

Table 3.3: Participatory wellbeing indicators

Mursi wellbeing indictors			
Indicators	Wellbeing Categories		
	Category 1	Category 2	Category 3
	lola (good life)	*kodgnogi* (Moderate life)	*Ropoga* (bad life)
Food /grain	3 – 4 storages (30 - 100kgs)	2 storages (10 100kgs)	Grain purchased; *godere, Nifro, possesi*
Assets			
- Livestock	Cattle 200; goat 120	Cattle 150; goat 40	None (orphan or widow) cannot marry
- tools			No working tools *konchera or* utensils *shirko*
Daughters	A good number	-	-
Education			
	Schooled	Schooled	-
Health	Family and animal health in good state	Family and animal health good	-

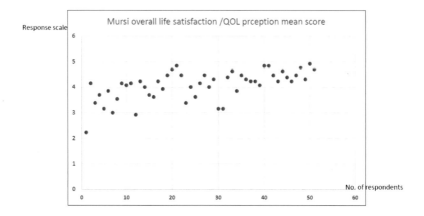

Figure 3.11: Perception of overall life satisfaction/QOL mean scores

3.10.1   *Material wellbeing (economic QOL)*

In order to understand the details of each domain response, we look at each response below is comparison with Fig. 3.12.

Under the material wellbeing category, regarding the basic needs met and level of income from tourism, the majority of respondents indicated satisfaction with both satisfaction of basic needs and income from tourism.

3.10.2   *Community wellbeing and emotional wellbeing (social and cultural QOL)*

Under the two domains of community wellbeing and emotional wellbeing, most local people in Mursi agreed on most of the social and cultural elements. For example, higher scores were given for local people's satisfaction with spiritual life, cultural preservation, leisure time, and security. The Mursi express the importance of their spiritual life and how their life is led by the Kumaru, a healer or kind of a priest, even to the point that if the period without rain is too long (they say there is a certain extent that is expected and tolerated), it was said that the Kumaru would do an exercise to help the Moon to pass to the west toward the Omo River, as it is when the Moon (*tobe*) does not pass to the west that the rain will not come. In this regard, the Mursi express that their life is dependent on their spiritual life.

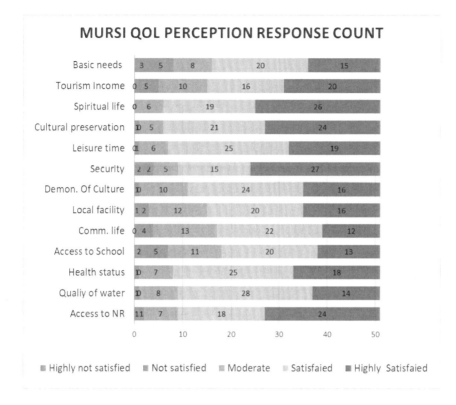

MURSI QOL PERCEPTION RESPONSE COUNT

	Highly not satisfied	Not satisfied	Moderate	Satisfaied	Highly Satisfaied
Basic needs	3	5	8	20	15
Tourism Income	0	5	10	16	20
Spiritual life	0	6	19		26
Cultural preservation	0	5	21		24
Leisure time	0	6	25		19
Securlty	2 2	5	15		27
Demon. Of Culture	0	10	24		16
Local facility	1 2	12	20		16
Comm. life	0 4	13	22		12
Access to School	2	5	11	20	13
Health status	0	7	25		18
Qualiy of water	0	8	28		14
Access to NR	11	7	18		24

*Highly not satisfied *Not satisfied *Moderate *Satisfaied *Highly Satisfaied

Figure 3.12: Perception of QOL response counts

3.10.3   Health and safety wellbeing (environmental QOL)

Under the health and safety wellbeing, the majority of Mursi showed satisfaction with access to natural resources, quality of water, and aspects of health status.

3.11   Economic, social, cultural, and environmental impacts of tourism

As part of their perception of QOL, a Likert-scale survey on the economic, social, cultural, and environmental impact of tourism was conducted, and the detailed responses are shown below (see detailed figures of each element in Annex V.B.1–7)

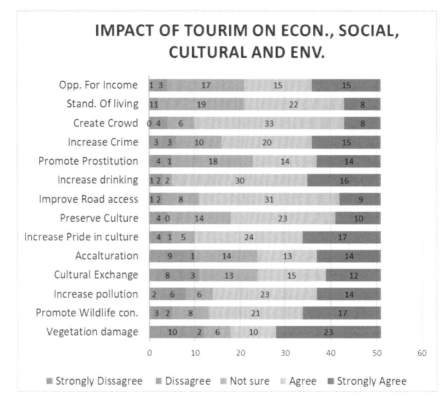

Figure 3.13: Perception of tourism impact response counts

3.11.1   Economic impacts of tourism

Regarding the economic impact of tourism, the majority of respondents agreed that tourism provides an opportunity for added income, which improves the standard of living. Although they valued tourism minimally in the qualitative survey of the benefits of tourism, they still agreed that income from tourism is important, however meager.

3.11.2   Social and cultural impacts of tourism

Regarding the social impact of tourism, a majority of the local people in Mursi agreed that tourism has negative impacts such as promoting drinking and prostitution and increasing crime and crowds. Similarly, the majority of Mursi people agreed on tourism's positive impact on improved road access in their area. The Mursi indicated that their one and only road access is very important, more than just as the means to bring tourists. They are also grateful for it provides access during an emergency.

Regarding the positive cultural impact of tourism, most local people in Mursi agreed that tourism increases cultural exchange, increases their pride in their culture, and preserves their culture. The Mursi also agreed that tourism has a negative impact on culture in its impact on acculturation.

3.11.3   *Positive and negative environmental impacts of tourism*

In the category of the negative environmental impacts of tourism, most Mursi agreed that tourism has a negative impact on vegetation, as well as a pollution impact. In this respect, the Mursi said that tourist cars cause some damage to vegetation. On the other hand, the majority of Mursi agree that tourism has also a positive impact on the preservation of wildlife and conservation, referring to the Mago National Park in the region.

3.12   Conclusion

This chapter examined one form of cultural tourism in the agro-pastoralist part of SOZ. This cultural tourism destination is one that has existed since the early 1970s in terms of tourist visits but, considering all types of early travelers and explorers, dates back into the 19th century. In this scenario, the main tourist interest is the Mursi women and girls with their cut lips and lip plates, a unique identity of the Mursi within the zone. However, all members of the Mursi are engaged in the tourist encounter. This tourist scenario's main feature can be termed "Photos for Cash," which is a transaction of cash for photos taken by the tourists. This type of tourist scenario is typical in all the pastoralist tourist destinations.

Tourist visits in this scenario are organized solely by the local guide. However, tourist visits are only allowed once payment is rendered to enter Mursi tourist sites, *orr touristi*. Still, the guide can determine the selection of tourist sites depending on their acquaintance with the members of different villages.

The Mursi, a transhumant society, move around to alternate their livelihood activities within the course of the year. They move between rain-fed and flood retread cultivation following the seasons. Tourist encounters are seemingly integrated into this movement between their two cultivation periods. Local people say that income from tourism provides cash mainly used to purchase grain in times of crop failure due to drought, rain variability, and pest infestations. As a result, it assists in maintaining their valuable asset, their cattle, which is their main asset to raise cash. Tourist encounters provide women access to and control over cash, which otherwise is not possible in the Mursi tradition. In Mursi, the sale of cattle is the husband's role, so women cannot have direct access to cash. Today, the cash they earn from tourists enables them to use it as they wish. In most cases, they use it to purchase grain in times of grain shortage, for medical purposes for their children in town, and, if they earn a good amount, to purchase cattle.

The Mursi people in the tourist destination still complain that the relationship with the guides is non-transparent. Sometimes the guides act as gatekeepers between the locals and the tourists. Furthermore, the Mursi at a tourist destination said that tourist income is still not sufficient to make a substantial life change. In a participatory wellbeing exercise, they scored the value of tourism's benefit at 2 out of 0–10. This shows their expected living standard, the level of wellbeing they wish to attain. During the qualitative interview, Mursi people at a tourist destination tended to report that tourism is a good opportunity to close a gap during times of vulnerability, such as drought and rain variability leading to crop failure; it is a means to maintain their valuable asset, their cattle, which normally is their insurance for raising cash in times of difficulty. Thus, they report at all times that it is good more than bad, an alternative means to raise cash: "*Touristi challi!*," tourists are good.

The local people's perception of their subjective wellbeing using a Likert scale showed an overall life satisfaction mean score of 4, "satisfied." Considering the participants' valuation of benefits from tourism, this is somewhat unexpected. However, during qualitative interviews, the Mursi people at tourist destinations always mentioned the inadequate level of tourist cash and benefit, as well as the low number of tourists coming to their site. They always say that no matter how meager the cash from tourists is, it is still invaluable.

CHAPTER 4

PARTICIPATORY OBSERVATION THROUGH PARTICIPATORY VISUAL RESEARCH METHODOLOGY (VRM)

4.1 Introduction

As part of the observation methodology, participatory visual research was conducted with the involvement of the local people from both research sites, that in Kebelle A in South Ari Woreda and that in Mursiland in Salamago Woreda. Four participants were taken as leads, and nine participants in total from both sites engaged in the exercise. All nine participants collectively produced 940 photographs and 10 pieces of video footage that depict the Ari and Mursi's life experiences in their respective locality.

4.1.1 Background and relevance

Virtual Research Methodology (VRM) involves research participants producing visual materials such as photography and/or film making that depicts local people's lives and life experiences in relation to their livelihood, in this instance in the SOZ, Southern Nations, Nationalities, and Peoples Region, Ethiopia. VRM using photography, videos, and other artwork has always been used in anthropology and sociology. However, lately, participatory VRM to produce new knowledge that involves research participants in producing their own material has become a new trend gaining interest among qualitative researchers (Buckingham, 2009; Gauntlet & Holzwarth, 2006; Rose, 2012; Shaw, 2017). Methodologies such as digital storytelling (DST) (Lambert, 2013) and autophotography, asking participants to take photographs of their environment and then using the photographs as actual data (Glaw et al., 2017) acknowledge participants as experts in their own lives (Shaw, 2017).

Beyond their gain in producing new knowledge into the academic dialogue, this type of creative activity also recognizes the values of the type of knowledge produced by the people themselves, which in turn are said to have therapeutic values for people involved in such methodology (Edwards, 2004).

The goal of these exercises was to engage the local people in creating their own narrative by reflecting their reality and making their perspective an important input into knowledge formation around their livelihood. It also specifically aims to understand the livelihood pattern of both settings, Kebelle A in South Ari Woreda and Mursiland in Salamago Woreda, and reveal the interface of tourism within their daily lives in both settings.

4.1.2   Methodology

Research participants in both sites were involved in taking footage with photos and film as observation data for the research, and as output to communicate their views at an exhibition for a larger public. Participants were free to select their scenes and themes to tell their own story in the style they planned it. It was also done in a way that respects and does not violate their sacred places, values, and rituals in any way. They were in full control of the extent that they display and the means of dissemination of their output. Therefore, in order to determine the respective procedures, prior consultations were made to reach a consensus on how outputs of their work could be released publicly. The consultation also continued at all stages to clarify a common understanding of the project and working modalities in order to mitigate misunderstandings and any challenges associated with VRM, as indicated by Shaw (2017).

To take such footage, two simple cameras were handed to the research site representatives leading the VRM, one camera each. The idea was to convince five people from each village to take photos and films by sharing the camera provided. Initially, the two representatives were both female; however, in Mursiland, the person responsible had to move to Jinka City; therefore, she handed it over to her male colleague. In order to support the participants' technical capacity, simple training was provided solely to teach participants how to handle and operate the camera. However, no technical know-how for producing quality photography or short film making was provided. By and large, local people in these areas are already acquainted with capturing images through their mobile phones, and in Mursiland, young girls are already well accustomed to the trend by age 15.

The exercise had the expected outcome of producing visual documentation in the form of photos, photobooks, and video clips to show the current status of local people's livelihood dynamics, knowledge, culture, and beliefs that determine their livelihood patterns, and the social and environmental relations in the formation of their livelihood. It also is expected to record the interface of the tourism activity within their livelihood and its impact. The exercise was also expected to generate ongoing dialogue among different stakeholders on such diverse issues as the role of tourism and understanding the role of social and natural environments in livelihood formation in the zone, cultural trends, and gender relations. As a means of sharing the results with the greater public, a local exhibition was planned in collaboration with a local university, Jinka University, and the South Omo Research Center Museum in Jinka.

4.2   VRM exercise

Nine people participated in the exercise, four men and five women. The majority of the partisans, four women and three men, were from Mursiland. The camera was given to both sites simultaneously and was left for the same period, February 2018 to August 2019. The exercise is still ongoing ,as both sites have retained the cameras they have been provided to take more footage.

In total, some 940 photographs were taken at both sites and 10 films were made with themes such as local festival in Jinka, local cattle treatment techniques in Mursi, children's games and playing styles in Mursi, and a local festival in Mursi. In August 2018, a one-day meeting was held at the SOZ research center in Jinka with participants to categorize and label all photos and films according to respective photographers. This was particularly necessary for the Mursi, as the vast preponderance of footage was from Mursiland.

4.2.1   *A preliminary screening of photos*

In December 2018, an informal and preliminary photo screening workshop was held at the African Area Studies, Kyoto University, to share the work that has been undertaken. In these viewing, the only purpose was to share photos that had been collected and acknowledge the people who took those photos and videos via PowerPoint.

4.2.2   *Staging an exhibition*

In August 2019, an exhibition was staged in collaboration with the University of Jinka and with the support of the African Area Studies, University of Kyoto, under the title "Through the Eyes Gazed" (Photo 4.1). SOZ Research Center and Kyoto Field Station, whose main role is the preservation of local cultural heritage also provided their support to ensure holding a successful exhibition.

Photo 4.1: "Through the Eyes Gazed" Exhibition day

4.2.3   Observation through VRM

During the research period of 2018–2019 research participants were involved in taking photographs and video footage. The aim was to enhance learning and see their perspective in terms of their way of life. This methodology has enabled me, as part of my observation, to note several issues.

1. The diverse potential of the cultural asset that "cultural tourism" is missing. In particular, in Mursiland, participants highlight the colorful and intricate livelihood style and pattern they are willing to share. During tourist visits, the duration that tourists take is not more than an hour to an hour and a half, which is mainly devoted to taking pictures of the Mursi people. This mainly focuses on the lip plates of women, which the Mursi ethnic group is known for. Tourists never attempt to understand or discover how the people live or their diverse traditional or cultural dimensions. It is very rare for tourists to camp or ask to stay in the villages, while the Mursi people are always puzzled why the people come in a hurry and leave in a hurry.

2. The photographs show implicitly and explicitly the authentic traditions of the group. Once again, this is highlighted in the Mursi ethnic group, who depicted images that are contrary to the majority of tourist photographs uploaded to the internet that one can access with the simple word of "Mursi photos." These photos are even portrayed as advertisements by major institutions like Ethiopian airlines promoting "the tribal south," depicting patterns of attire, body decorations, and adornments that are not consistent with the authentic traditions of the ethnic group. During an interview regarding this, one Mursi mother said:

The tourists ask us to put stuff on before taking pictures. We think that they all like this stuff, so we put them, so they take our picture and give us money ... Otherwise, this is not our culture. (Interview with women focus group discussion, August 2019)

This is evidenced by some major international photographers who have made coffee table books depicting the Mursi in dramatic and hideous positions, and have also involved children who are asked to pose in different positions whose purposes in demonstrating the cultural values of the ethnic group are not clear (Photo 4.2). In particular, what is the understanding of the photographers? Are they simply trying to make seemingly "exotic" pictures to sell their photographs, even knowing that they are not actually representative of their culture? Or were they misled by informants, believing that it is the way of their culture? Another sad thing is those people even do not know that their faces are sold for many millions that the photographers earn freely. Or do they pay royalties to the government? This can be another issue for research.

Photo 4.2: Comparison of Mursi and professional photos

3. The capability of photography and video taking of the local people even without technical training in photography and videography is astounding. The photos taken are of very high quality and worthy of exhibit.

4. The themes that they have chosen to express in pictures tell stories and the group's way of life. Photographs highlight gender roles, including women's diverse roles. The heavy burden of women in child-rearing, along with their daily chores such as milling, water, and firewood collection; early morning milking, making their family hut, and in between posing for tourists to earn cash (see Table

4.1). Also, themes such as tourism encounters, culture, livelihood, people, food, and coffee ceremony gatherings can be observed.

Elfnesh – South   Ari

Natuy - Mursi

Bardole - Mursi

Teraboshi - Mursi

Bardole - Mursi

Elfnesh – South Ari

Photo 4.3: Selected photos
Source: Selected Participatory Visual Research outcome

CHAPTER 5

COMPARATIVE ASSESSMENT OF THE TWO CASE STUDIES

5.1   Introduction

This chapter will outline the comparative study of the two case studies, that in Chapter Two of Kebelle A, South Ari, and in Chapter Three of Mursiland in Salamago Woreda in SOZ, illustrating local people's livelihood strategies when engaged in cultural tourism. The comparison will be based on selected variables from the livelihood framework, the wellbeing assessment, and the Likert-scale outcomes on quality of life and the economic, social, cultural, and environmental impact of tourism. In addition, a comparison will be made of the two life story accounts following a livelihood concept approach.

The variables selected for comparison are assets that have created an opportunity for cultural tourism in both of the case site units, the types of drivers that necessitate diversification, gender aspects in relation to cultural tourism as a livelihood strategy, responses to the valuation of tourism in comparison to wellbeing aspiration, overall quality of life results, and the economic, social, cultural, and environmental impacts of tourism.

5.1.1   Assets for livelihood strategy in cultural tourism

People in Kebelle A are in close contact with tourists due to their proximity to Jinka Town, the hub for most tourism coming to the Zone. As there is also a lodge in the vicinity, and the market in Jinka town, tourist flow is regular in the area. However, the Ari people were not engaged in tourism activities directly until members of a local guide took the initiative to interest tourists on their way to other tourist destinations, usually in the agro-pastoralist woredas. Kebelle A was one of those selected that joined the initiative.

In Kebelle A, local people took the opportunity to offer tourists their skills and local knowledge systems based on the Ari people's life experiences, culture, and traditions. This enabled selected people in Kebelle A to engage in the cultural tourism started by the local guide group starting in 2012. Selected households with the skill and knowledge of crafts and local food and beverage preparation, which mostly served as their means of livelihood, are targeted to join the initiative, which created an opportunity to access alternative livelihood and income.

In Mursiland, early records of travelers in the territory were recorded from the end of the nineteenth century. According to local informants, tourism started in the 1960s. The Mursi were shy toward new visitors up until the late 1990s, but gradually developed their photogenic behavior.

In Mursiland, local people's cultural identity, which includes women's and girl's lip cutting and lip plates, which were normally cultural rituals for girls to transition into adulthood and a mark of their identity, are their distinguishing feature and the basis for their engagement in cultural tourism. As a result, since the early 70s, the local people have taken the opportunity to earn cash in a tourism scenario of "photos for cash."

5.1.2   Social assets

In Kebelle A, social relations and networks are considered an important factor in making it in life, as participants elaborated during a focus group discussion. Local people's engagement in cultural tourism is also based on the quality of and acquaintance with the guide association, in addition to possessing the skills and knowledge of the activities to be exhibited to the tourists. Local people in Kebelle A feel that they are at the mercy of the guide association. However, they are not proactive in finding ways to gain access to tourist visits free from the guide association's control. In some instances, because of conflicts between local youth in the area and the guide association, tourist visits were discontinued, and the local people felt penalized for reasons not of their own doing.

For people in Mursiland, where the guide creates the opportunity to link to tourism activity, their social networking ability is also important. As a result, the quality of their relationships and acquaintance is critical to secure tourist visits to their sites in competition with other tourist sites in the area. This, however, is resented by the local people in Mursi, as the guides possess the ultimate power to regulate tourist visits in their area. As a result, they have made numerous demands of the local office and a direct request that the local zonal tourism office mediate and facilitate an equitable distribution of tourist visits. Consequently, the zone office has written a letter instructing guide associations working in Mursiland to ensure that all tourist visits are distributed fairly.

Mobile phones are an important device in creating contact and receiving regular alerts of tourist movements in both sites.

5.1.3   Relationships with institutions and organizations

Local people have a love-hate relationship with the guide association. Tourist visits are mainly arranged by the guides, so local people maintain good relationships with the guides at all time. However the benefit sharing of the scheme lacks transparency and accountability on the part of the guide association, which creates great resentment among the local people in Kebelle A. In 2017, an interview with the Kebelle administrator revealed that their knowledge of the initiative is very minimal and not official, so they do not maintain formal contact with the people. As a result, the engagement of the local people in the tourism initiative is informal. This has created a difficult situation for the people in Kebelle A to negotiate with the youth guide regarding payment, on benefit-sharing, and work ethics. The local people who receive tourists lack the confidence to demand their rightful claim for what is due them; they are vulnerable and powerless. The local people are now the tourist's main attraction point, thereby creating employment and economic benefits even if absent from the official tourism structure.

In Mursi, locals have instituted a tourist payment scheme where tourists have to pay prior to their entry into the village to take photos. The Mursi people themselves regulate this system of benefit sharing.

Local authorities regulating tourist activity in the zone and woreda have no direct link with local people at the destination in Mursiland. To some extent, this can be seen as neglectful by local authority, whereby local people are ignored and without any support. However, according to the local authority, local people from Mursi have recently made several visits to demand better working of the guide association and have even written a letter asking that the visits of tourists be fair and regulated. As a result, a letter was written to all guide association insisting that they visit all sites equally and fairly.

At the zonal level, tourism is one focus in the area of youth employment as constituting a major opportunity for the government to combat unemployment. As a result, the local government maintains close contact with the youths and provides regular follow-ups, even providing training and including them in meetings regarding the sector's activities. This type of interaction does not happen with local people at the destination in Kebelle A or Mursiland. This amounts to neglect of the local people who are directly involved in the tourism activity by the local authorities, which has also been highlighted in Tomaselli (2015).

5.1.4   Drivers of livelihood diversification

Kebelle A, predominantly an agrarian population, has recently been transforming into an urban society. With the fragmentation of land due to population pressure, coupled with young peoples' decreased interest in the sector, the majority population has already started seeking alternative means of livelihood, thus accelerating the urban transformation. Moreover, their agrarian livelihood is highly affected by the effects of external shocks such as rain variability and pests, which drive crop price fluctuations that exacerbate local people's livelihood vulnerability. At the local level, people's lack of basic services such as water and electricity affects their livelihoods at the household level and their businesses.

Thus, seeking alternative livelihoods to address their vulnerability is imperative. Local people say that tourism was expected to provide the opportunity to alleviate their daily cash needs. However, the way it currently works is not offering the expected level of benefit.

The Mursi people at the destination, still agro-pastoralists, are dependent on their grain cultivation and livestock rearing. The slow onset drought, recurrent external shocks such as rain variability and pests make their livelihoods precarious. In addition, pressure from government policies that affect their land and flood plains has added to the challenges of their livelihood. Still, as a transhumant society, they move around looking for a better place to make their life meaningful. From the early 1990s until today, their land has further shrunk, as major flood-retreat cultivable land has been appropriated for major commercial farms for national and international companies, as well as national government sugar plantations and sugar factories. Yet, the Mursi people and their neighboring ethnic groups have not been appropriately consulted on any of these measures, and appropriate forms of compensation or alternative means of livelihood have not been developed. Rather, a villagization program strongly contrary to their lifestyle is being pushed without their consent to settle them as a sedentary society. The sugar factory claims to have prepared for each household 0.75 ha of land as a plantation area in the sugar plantation and 0.25 ha for maize plantation for their consumption when they settle. This, however, is not implemented unless they settle.

At the local level, the global effects of climate change, driving drought, rain variability, and pest infestation, have affected the Mursi livelihood; however, because of their ownership of cattle, which can be sold to buy grain during drought and difficult situations, they receive the least government assistance of any group in the area. According to Turton (1995) the Mursi own the smallest herds per capita among the region's pastoralist communities, and their herds are more than just insurance; they also serve important social functions such as the brides' wealth. As a result, selling their cattle is a last resort. The Mursi in the tourist destination areas showed harsh realities of hunger and destitution during interviews and personal observations all throughout my fieldwork in 2017–2019.

5.1.5   *Cash utilization*

As cash earning in Kebelle A is manipulated by the guides, with delayed payments or even non-payment, the amount earned is often meager. Still, local people revealed that cash earned from tourists is usually used to purchase food items. In a survey to assess the use of cash from tourism in all the households engaged in tourism in Kebelle A, 90% of the people reported using cash to purchase food items. In the case of substantial earnings, local people said that they use cash to strengthen their businesses.

In Mursi, local people also use cash from tourists to purchase grain/flour in times of grain production failure. In an interview of 39 people at the Mursi research site, 22 (59%) respondents said they spend cash to purchase food items (grain/flour). In the same interview, 10 people (26%) said they spend it on medical expenses. These are in the age categories between 19–80 years, making up 32 of the 39 people interviewed in total. Younger respondents, aged 15–18, said that they spend their cash on jewelry and utensils.

Tourist cash also allows them to maintain their valuable asset, their livestock. Today, they substitute cash from tourists for livestock sales to purchase grain or raise cash for other needs such as medical expenses. This is considered a major benefit for the Mursi people, as livestock is an important asset, which they prefer to avoid selling for future risk management and to maintain their asset, as it is important in their social practice.

5.1.6   *Gender aspects and cultural tourism*

In Kebelle A, the majority of selected households involved in tourism activities are headed by women. This is mainly due to the nature of the work they perform for their livelihood. Most are artisans engaged in pottery and local food and beverage production. Also, these activities are a means for most women to start a livelihood, particularly female-headed households. In this case, the guide association in South Ari targeted those engaged in pottery, food, and beverage production to showcase their work to tourists as examples of people's local life, experience, culture, and tradition. This has created an opportunity for women to capitalize their capabilities and create additional income for those already struggling in a vulnerable situation. The women appreciate this tourism activity, as they do not have to engage in any extra activity to earn cash from tourists. This is advantageous for women to continue working to engage in their daily lives, and creates extra opportunities to diversify their income.

For local people in Mursiland, tourist visits are mainly driven by the cultural features of the women and girls in Mursi because of their lip cuts and lip plates. Thus, the women are highly engaged in the tourist encounter. Their engagement has created a unique opportunity for access to cash, which normally was in the hands of men/husbands, who traditionally handle cash in Mursi.

Today, women and girls alike are earning cash from tourists and, most importantly, have the liberty to use it in any way they like with full control. They mostly use it to purchase grain and cover medical expenses. They also purchase flour to ease the drudgery of milling grain.

However, in Mursi, women as the lead cultivators move from their two cultivation sites throughout the year following a seasonal schedule. The encounter with tourists also requires moving to a different site to meet the tourists, which therefore adds an extra move for women from their cultivation sites, adding to the burden in their already heavy schedule of productive and reproductive roles.

5.1.7   Life stories

Here we reflect on the life stories of two women in the case study areas, following their livelihood trajectories to examine certain elements with regard to the intentionality and strategic behavior of the actors throughout their life stories.

E.K.'s life was one of turmoil at an early age, with war, displacement, and a new beginning in a far country after the loss of her father. She believes that her dropping out of school due to hunger pangs from not having enough to eat changed her life course, while her brother, who coped better, finished school and succeeded in life: He has become a government employee and leads a better life. Her struggle continued, being abducted at an early age, divorced, and left as a single mother. She engages in a trade that she is familiar with, making *areke*, which she learned from her mother, to survive. Still, the effort she puts in is not enough to change her livelihood.

Tourist cash was sought as an opportunity to supplement her livelihood, but she says it is still a struggle. The guide association that introduced the scheme is not trustworthy in handing over her due earnings, and as a result the cash she earns is close to none.

In Mursi, G.W. recollects harsh times due to war, disease, and famine. It was a life that requires moving to make a living, and in good times, she says, everything is in their surroundings. The role of women, as cultivators, is difficult, particularly during the dry season when water is scarce.

She states that her first tourist encounter was during a famine crisis where food aid was being distributed at a place called Dilldili. Since then, she has participated in tourist encounters to make extra cash. Today she said that they earn cash from tourists of up to 500 ETB/day, but points out that the guides interfere with the tourist flow among tourist sites.

In both settings the women recall war and conflict that defined their harsh lives. Their main livelihood is also challenged due to external shocks that negatively impact their livelihood, putting their lives in a dire situation. In both stories, tourism is sought as an alternative means of livelihood, giving the opportunity to use their cultural assets to earn cash, yet both complain about the relationship with the guide association that plays an important role in bringing tourists to their sites. Both women expressed the powerlessness they experienced in both settings from the unfair business deals made by the guide associations.

5.1.8   *Comparison of the qualitative tourist benefit valuation and quality of life survey results*

A qualitative and participatory wellbeing indicator identification exercise was conducted during focus group discussions. In Kebelle A, nine participants engaged in identifying their wellbeing indicators in terms of the good life (*mitchu hiwot* in Amharic, *dokintoiyo uste* in Ari), under which term they divided the state of the good life into three categories. Wellbeing, *dokintiyo uste/michu hiwot*, meaning a good life or comfortable life, is the first category; *mers lekmyo*, which is a medium level of wellbeing, is the second; and *kin tstskiye* (*yaltemmuala hiwot* in Amharic), an unfulfilled life, is the third. In this regard, participants identified nine indicators that characterized the three categories: Food availability (both quality and quantity); Housing; Assets, as in household goods, *era ziga;* Family Life; Social Network; Savings; Education; and Health. The participants then undertook an exercise assessing tourist benefit with respect to their aspired wellbeing. They rated the benefit from tourism at 3 on a range of 0–10.

In the case of perception of QOL/life satisfaction, responses of 51 participants were scored on four domains: Material Wellbeing, Community wellbeing, Emotional Wellbeing and Health, and Safety Wellbeing, using 13 items (questions) scored on a five-point Likert scale ranging from *highly dissatisfied* (1), *not satisfied* (2), *moderate* (3), and *satisfied* (4) to *highly satisfied* (5). Accordingly, the overall QOL/life satisfaction of local people in Kebelle A showed a mean score of 3, which indicates moderate life satisfaction on the response scale.

The same exercise identifying qualitative wellbeing indicators was undertaken in Mursiland. Accordingly, wellbeing/quality of life was identified as *lola*. The FGD participants categorized *lola* into three categories: The good life as *lukuma, delleley*, or *danka*; a moderate category, *kadgnogi*; and *ropga*, a bad life. These categories then were characterized with five indicators: Food quantity, assets, number of daughters, education, and health. Accordingly, the valuation of tourism benefits was based on the local peoples' aspirations for their wellbeing. The result showed that local people from Mursi rated the benefit from tourism at 2 on a range of $0 - 10$.

The quality of life/life satisfaction survey in Mursi involving 51 respondents yielded a mean overall life satisfaction score of 4, which is within the "satisfied" category. Here also, the score diverges from the qualitative results regarding the benefit of tourism. In the valuation exercise, the only focus was the benefit of tourism in local people's wellbeing, evaluated in relation to the wellbeing indicator they have identified and the extent to which it satisfies their expectations. At both research sites local people have valued the benefit from tourism at a fairly low level, showing that the benefit received from tourism is not at this stage adequate to satisfy their aspired level of wellbeing.

In the case of the QOL questionnaires, local people in Kebelle A responded to both questions reported themselves not satisfied regarding not only the economic aspect of tourism performance but also its social, cultural, and environmental aspects. On the other hand, local people from Mursi responded to both questions that they were satisfied. This made a difference in the overall QOL result.

5.1.9   *Comparison of the economic, social, cultural, and environmental impacts of tourism*

In this section we compare the responses to the Likert-scored questions, taking *strongly disagree* and *disagree* as one category, "disagree," and *agree* and *strongly agree* as another category, "agree," avoiding the middle response of *not sure*.

5.1.9.1   *Economic impacts of tourism*

Kebelle A respondents disagreed that tourism provides income opportunity and that it improves the standard of living. This may be attributable to their disappointment with the style of benefit sharing in Kebelle A, where the guide takes full control of tourists' cash, depriving local people of their due income.

However, in Mursi, local people agreed that tourism gives them income opportunity and improves living standards. In this case, the managed benefit sharing and payment arrangement in Mursiland may have contributed to a positive perception.

5.1.9.2   *Social impacts of tourism*

Regarding its social impact, local people in Kebelle A disagreed that tourism improves road access, complaining that the quality of their only road has not changed since it was constructed, so they do not see its impact as improving road quality. On the other hand, local people from Mursi agreed that tourism improves road access, indicating that the only access road that tourists use to visit them has also provided access during emergencies.

Regarding the same element of social impact, the local people from Kebelle A disagreed that tourism has a negative impact on social issues, as by promoting drinking, prostitution, or crime, or increasing crowds in the village. Contrariwise, local people in Mursi agreed that tourism has such negative impacts as increased drinking, prostitution, crime, and crowds during tourist visits.

5.1.9.3   *Cultural impacts of tourism*

Regarding its cultural impacts, local people in Kebelle A agreed on all positive impacts of tourism on culture, such as its effect in increasing pride in their culture and promoting the preservation of their culture, except that regarding the exchange of culture, they did not believe that they experienced any cultural exchange from the tourist side. In terms of the negative impact of tourism on culture, they disagreed that tourism has an impact on acculturation.

In Mursi, local people similarly agreed on all positive impacts except cultural exchange, and for similar reasons as in Kebelle A. However, Mursi local people agreed that tourism has an impact on acculturation.

5.1.9.4   *Environmental impacts of tourism*

Regarding its environmental impacts, the majority of respondents in Kebelle A disagreed that tourism damages vegetation and increases pollution, but agreed that it has a positive impact on wildlife conservation, indicating the Protected Area of Mago National Park. The Mursi people, on the other hand, agreed that tourism has a negative impact in damaging vegetation and increasing pollution, but also agreed that it has a positive impact on wildlife conservation, similarly indicating Mago National Park.

The divergent responses in the two-tourist scenario may reflect the stages of tourism in the two case study areas.

The Kebelle A tourist initiative, a newly started initiative, is still at the stage of figuring out how to manage the relationship with the guides and tourists. Among the Mursi, because of their long-term experience with tourism, the system and relationships of the local people with the different stakeholders are to some extent managed in ways favorable to the local people. In scenarios where locals have a grievance, they are also confident in being able to manage it, for example, by making contact with the local authorities to improve the distribution of tourist visits to tourist sites. In Kebelle A, they are still not clear how to go beyond the stage of dependency on the guide association. Even the proximity of Kebelle A to the city has not made a difference in approaching local authorities involved in the matter, such as the tourism office.

The relationships with different stakeholders in the two tourist scenarios can be associated with the concept of the tourism life cycle model of Butler (1980), in which a tourism scenario is created based on the stages of tourism, of which six stages are posited, starting with the exploration stage and developing into the involvement stage, the development stage, the consolidation stage, the stagnation stage, and the rejuvenation stage. According to Butler (1980), tourist areas in the early stage involve a small number of tourists and local people without much of a significant impact on the economic or social aspects of their lives. Then, gradually, as facilities increase and awareness of the area increases, visitors also grow in number. Eventually, development reaches the stagnation level or decline stage, after the area's carrying capacity reach its limit and resources to accommodate new visitors get scarce. As this stage reaches its peak level, local people will start to notice the negative sides of tourism more than its benefits. These might include land, water, transportation, accommodation, and services, among other factors. As a result, tourism activity will stagnate until either a new strategy is devised to rejuvenate the sector or it completely drops out of the tourism market. In this scheme, the tourism stage in Kebelle A, being a new initiative, can be said to be at a stage of exploration, where small numbers of tourists discover the site, with a primary tourist attraction of natural and cultural elements in line with Butler's (1980) description. As a result, tourism's impact on economic or social aspects is insignificant to the local people. On the other hand, we can say comparatively that the local people in the Mursi tourism scenario, which has been continuing since the 70s, have started to recognize these negative impacts. Still, the scenario is not in the full development stage as described by Butler (1980), and as a result the local people still aspire for more tourist visits, even with the impacts they feel.

5.2   Conclusion

The local people in the two case research areas face comparable precarious livelihood patterns due to recurrent external shocks such as rain variability, pest infestation impacting their livelihood. Still, they have transcended challenges and are resilient and will continue in the face of changing reality. Today, Kebelle A is quickly converting into an urban setting, which eventually will transform into a fully-fledged part of Jinka Town. The Mursi people are still struggling between the government's push for them to convert into a sedentary society and their desire to maintain their agro-pastoral system.

In both case study settings, cultural tourism is providing livelihood opportunities to the local people at the destination, but not to such a level that it can dramatically change their living standard, according to their own evaluation. Still, their engagement continues, and the activity is informal given the government's indifferent attitude. The tourism sector at the zonal and woreda level is sought after as a major area for creating employment for youth, but it stops there. The people who are the tourists' main interest and the major pull factor for the tourism sector itself are never given attention to support them and see that their needs are addressed. This is contrary to the values promoted in the national sustainable tourism master plan in terms of community participation and empowerment elaborated in the introduction of this document under the policy review section.   From this, it is easy to deduce that the highly praised tourism sector has a long way to go in meeting the socio-economic need of the local people at cultural tourist destinations.

CHAPTER 6

CONCLUSION

This research, provides a distinct view of cultural tourism in terms of its significance towards livelihood and wellbeing from local peoples` perspective to understand the extent of benefit beyond cash earnings for local people at destination by examining their detailed livelihood patterns using the sustainable livelihood approach (Scoones, 2009). This illuminates how tourism as an activity is integrated within their livelihood strategy mix, identifying assets and bases that create an opportunity for livelihood in cultural tourism and the drivers that lead local people to seek cultural tourism as a diversification livelihood strategy. Furthermore, it also assesses the effect on their wellbeing of their engagement in tourism activities, first through a participatory exercise that identified local wellbeing indicators and valuations of tourism benefits in relation to local people's outlined wellbeing aspiration, and then through a survey to assess the local people's subjective perception of their wellbeing.

Following the sustainable livelihood framework, the tourism livelihood strategy can be expressed as a means of delivery of income to local people that has enabled them to close a gap in their livelihood and maintain their assets. This, according to local people's perspective, is conveyed as, even if meager and unevenly distributed, benefit from tourism actively contributed towards their wellbeing in the form of food security, health security, and asset building. In terms of sustainability, it has demonstrated the capability of local people to adapt to internal stress and external shocks, strengthening their resilience. In particular, highlighted their inherent knowledge systems and their cultural assets providing the means to adapt in vulnerable situations.

In conclusion outlined under the following three elements and elaborated in detail. Finally, a brief recommendation is advanced.

6.1   Comparative analysis

This research had undertaken a comparative case study on two cultural tourist scenarios to understand significance of tourism on local peoples` livelihood and wellbeing taking a livelihood approach framework as analysis. Comparison is then made based on a number of variables following the livelihood approach such as identifying assets for livelihood building, role of institutions and organizations, types of drivers for diversification into tourism as a strategy, tourist cash utilization. It has also taken a qualitative and quantitative approach to look into the effect of cultural tourism on local peoples` wellbeing in terms of their perspective. It also looked into how local people understand the impact of tourism on factors such as economic, social, cultural, and the environment through a Likert-scale survey in both sites. Brief details on the comparison are discussed as follows.

In the two cultural tourism scenarios, two different types of cultural asset bases create opportunity livelihood strategies. In Kebelle A, their skills and local knowledge systems are assets that have created an opportunity to access alternative livelihoods that create income. In Mursi, their cultural identity, that is, women's and girls' lip cutting and plates, constitutes an important base in tourism, creating a livelihood opportunity.

At both case sites, their social assets such as networking quality and acquaintance with the guide association play an important role in creating access to livelihood opportunities in tourism. As the sole contact, the guide association has the power to limit or facilitate tourist visits to both sites.

As well as access to tourist visits, local guide associations have full control over the earnings from tourists in the case of Kebelle A; therefore, their cash earning is manipulated so as to greatly reduce the earning of local people. In the case of local people from Mursi, this matter is better handled, as the payment of tourists always happens before tourists can enter the villages. All payments for photos are also made directly to the people involved.

This kind of management is not known by the local authorities regulating tourist activity in the zone within the structure of cultural tourism. They have no direct link with local people at the destinations, nor do they have any engagement with the activity that takes place at the destination. As a result, the local people are left on their own amounting to relevant governmental organizations and local authorities neglect, thus exposing the local people to direct abuse.

Apart from the past and present external shock factors and economic and policy trends in the region contributing to the local people's vulnerability, local people at both research sites report current external factors such as rain variability, pests, and price fluctuations as the main determinants for diversifying their livelihood strategies. In Kebelle A internal stress as in limited access to basic services such access to water and energy as in diminishing natural resources due to the expanding urbanization, as well as external shocks such as rain variability, and pest infestation drive local people to diversify their cash access to manage their daily household consumption and successfully manage their small business.

At both case study sites; tourist cash is mainly used to purchase food items as a form of coping. In Kebelle A, if a good amount is earned, which is very rare, local people said they use it to strengthen their businesses. In Mursi, local people use it to purchase grain/flour due to the recurrent crop shortage; in addition, cash from tourists is substituted to avoid selling their livestock to maintain their valuable asset base, their livestock, which is crucial to their livelihood but also helps them maintain their social functions. This has been their main purpose in pursuing tourist cash.

Cultural tourism affords women access to cash at both case study sites. In Kebelle A, it also capitalizes existing capabilities to create an opportunity for extra cash earning without any additional effort. Women in Mursi lessen their burden of drudgery as the cash is used to purchase flour, reducing grain milling. However, it was observed that the extra movement involved in engaging in tourist encounters could impose an added burden on women in Mursi alongside their productive and reproductive roles.

Comparison of qualitative tourist benefit valuations and a quantitative quality of life survey based on a Likert-scale questionnaire yielded different results at the two case study sites. In Kebelle A, local people valued tourist benefit at 3 on a range of 0–10 and in Mursi at 2. These results are based on local people's aspired wellbeing, which they identified through a participatory exercise in a focus group discussion. In this valuation, the divergent outcome can be explained by the fact that criteria of wellbeing can be different for different people and in different places, as Chambers and Conway (1992) have indicated. At the same time, the manner benefit sharing is handled in both sites may have an effect on how they have valued benefit.

In the case of perception of overall QOL/life satisfaction, local people in Kebelle A showed an average mean score of 3, indicating moderate satisfaction. The same survey found a mean overall life satisfaction/QOL score for the local people in Mursi of 4, which is satisfactory. Here also, the scores show divergent results.

In the valuation exercise, the only factor was the benefit of tourism to local people. In the process, participants evaluated the benefit from tourism in relation to the wellbeing they aspired to in relation to the indicator they identified through the participatory exercise in the focus group discussion. In the case of the QOL questionnaires, not only the economic aspects of tourism performance but also the social, cultural, and environmental aspects were reflected in their QOL scores.

The economic aspect, as one domain, had two questions: satisfaction with the fulfillment of basic needs and satisfaction with income from tourism, where local people, from Kebelle A, responded to both questions as not satisfied. On the other hand, local people from Mursi responded to both questions as satisfied. This clearly made a difference in the overall QOL result of both research sites.

In terms of tourism perception of tourism impact on economic, social, cultural and environmental factors responses to the Likert-scale questions are reported in two catagroies. The *strongly disagree* and *disagree* as one category, and *agree* and *strongly agree* as another category, avoiding the middle response of *not sure* is used to demonstrate the tendency of local people's responses towards their perception on the tourism impact.

The majority of local people in Kebelle A disagreed that tourism affords them income opportunities and improves the standard of living; however, in Mursi most agreed that tourism gives them income opportunities and improves their standard of living. In this case, the managed benefit sharing and payment arrangement in Mursiland might have created a higher level of satisfaction.

In terms of social impact, most local people in Kebelle A disagreed that tourism improves road access, complaining that the quality of their only road has not changed since it was constructed, so they do not see its impact as improving road quality. On the other hand, local people from Mursi agreed that tourism improves road access, indicating that the only access road that tourists use to visit them has also provided access during emergencies. Looking into negative impacts on social factors, the local people from Kebelle A disagreed that tourism has a negative impact on social issues, as by promoting drinking, prostitution, or crime, or increasing crowds in the village. Contrariwise, local people in Mursi agreed that tourism has such negative impacts as increased drinking, prostitution, crime, and crowds during tourist visit.

In regard to cultural impacts, local people in Kebelle A agreed on all positive impacts of tourism on culture, such as its effect in increasing pride in their culture and promoting the preservation of their culture, except that regarding the exchange of culture, they did not believe that they experienced any cultural exchange from the tourist side. In terms of the negative impact of tourism on culture, they disagreed that tourism has an impact on acculturation. In Mursi, local people similarly agreed on all positive impacts except cultural exchange, and for similar reasons as in Kebelle A. However, Mursi local people agreed that tourism has an impact on acculturation.

On questions of environmental impacts, the majority of respondents in

Kebelle A disagreed that tourism damages vegetation and increases pollution, but agreed that it has a positive impact on wildlife conservation, indicating the Protected Area of Mago National Park. The Mursi people, on the other hand, agreed that tourism has a negative impact in damaging vegetation and increasing pollution, but also agreed that it has a positive impact on wildlife conservation, similarly indicating Mago National Park.

The divergent responses in the two-tourist scenario may reflect the stages of tourism in the two case study areas. The Kebelle A tourist initiative, a newly started initiative, is still at the stage of figuring out how to manage the relationship with the guides and tourists. Among the Mursi, because of their long-term experience with tourism, the system and relationships of the local people with the different stakeholders are to some extent managed in ways favorable to the local people. In scenarios where locals have a grievance, they are also confident in being able to manage it, for example, by making contact with the local authorities to improve the distribution of tourist visits to tourist sites. In Kebelle A, they are still not clear how to go beyond the stage of dependency on the guide association. Even the proximity of Kebelle A to the city has not made a difference in approaching local authorities involved in the matter, such as the tourism office.

6.2   Cultural capital as an opportunity to address vulnerability

In Chapter 2, local people in Kebelle A were described as depending on their skills, local knowledge system, and cultural capabilities were conceived of as elements of intangible cultural assets to present to tourists and introduced as cultural and traditional elements of the Ari community. Like other sites, tourists do not just visit the local people, but those visited have skills that they can show and explain to the tourists, so that their activity provides them an opportunity to participate in the initiative. This then creates the means for them to make extra income to close a gap in their livelihood. In Chapter 3, we saw that for the local people in Mursi, their identity and in particular women's special features of lip cutting and lip plates are a major attraction for tourists. This unique feature has been one asset/capital that the Mursi people have been able to draw an advantage from to receive additional income for their livelihood. They attest that this provides valuable input in safeguarding the main livelihood asset that the Mursi safeguard most, their livestock. Cash from a tourist is quick money they can use to purchase grain in times of grain failure or purchase medicine for children and adults, utensils, and cattle. In Mursi, as a tourist visits the whole village, no separation is made between people. In fact, men also have the opportunity to make money by posing for a photo, as do children and young boys.

As a result, although the SLF does not classify a cultural asset explicitly as one asset in the framework, Scoones (2009) leaves room to include more assets. In this study, therefore, I include cultural capital as identified by Throsby (2003) as one asset/capital that local people in the two cultural tourism destinations have used to create an alternative livelihood strategy.

This is demonstrated in both research case sites, where they take the opportunity offered by an asset/capital that is at hand to make a meaningful addition to their livelihood. This is a reflection of their agency to use all available means to supplement their livelihood (Chambers & Conway, 1992). Also, as Bebbington (1999) stated, assets are vehicles for action (making a living), hermeneutic action (making living meaningful), and emancipatory action (challenging the structures under which one makes a living). In Mursi, G.W., a mother, testifies to having abandoned her rain-fed cultivation, as the rain is too unreliable to depend on compared to what she can get from tourists. This seems to indicate that the Mursi have made a trade-off of their cultivation for tourist cash, even if cultivation offers a better return. Still, as its risk potential is higher, they chose to wait on tourists for cash, however meager, as the risk is minimal.

6.3   Recommendations

6.3.1   An incentive-based cultural tourism option

From this case study research, the overall understanding is that local people at the destination are engaged in tourism activities. However, everything that happens is haphazardly conducted in an effort to seize the opportunity to meaningfully supplement their livelihood.

The benefit they receive is not significant according to their own evaluations. However, any benefit they receive is critical for their vulnerable livelihood, showing the needs they must meet. Local people's engagement in cultural tourism is mainly in pursuit of livelihood opportunities; thus, local authorities and policymakers need to study how to address the basic needs of the local people. Providing an incentive to people at the destination to address their basic needs considering their important role in the sector's objectives can lead local people to engage in tourism activities with dignity and promote a two-way cultural exchange between tourists and people at the tourist destination. This is illustrated in the schematic (Figure 6.1).

The zonal local authority is clearly not equipped to engage with the local people and understand their needs and the shortcomings at the destination. This was also clearly indicated by zonal and woreda local authorities regarding their limited capacity and clear mandate on how to engage with local people at the destination. The general direction of the activities of zonal offices is to support the people already engaged in the tourism sector, especially the youth, as this is considered the best option for addressing unemployment in the area. Beyond that, there is no strategy to address the needs of local people at the destination who constitute the main attraction of tourists at destination. It is therefore important for local authorities at the local level to pay attention to cultural tourism destinations that engage local people directly. Local people at such destinations need to be closely monitored with respect to their socio-economic needs and the cultural aspects of their engagement in tourism activities.

6.3.2   *Environmental degradation and pollution*

Local people are taking advantage of their cultural assets as an opportunity to access improved livelihood; however, the cultural asset itself needs proper attention and protection. So far, there is no clear direction in the way of organizational support to preserve and conserve cultural assets. It is clear that local people have their own ways of preserving and protecting their cultural assets. However, governments need also provide support to protecting local culture in close collaboration with the local people where there is a direct threat to cultural assets. In this line, Throsby (1999) has pointed out that the parallels between natural and cultural capital, where similar to how overuse of exhaustible natural resources may cause systems break down, so can neglect of cultural capital by allowing deterioration and failure to sustain cultural values that provide people with sense of identity, not undertaking the investment required to maintain stock of intangible cultural capital leading into cultural systems to break down so the loss of welfare and economic output. The cultural tourism scenario in both the case study areas also demonstrate threat to cultural assets, in particular in the case of the Mursi case study where local peoples` perception of the impact of tourism on culture was reflected as negative. Thus, relevant institutions need to balance between the need of the local community to enhance their livelihood and preserving their cultural assets on the other end.

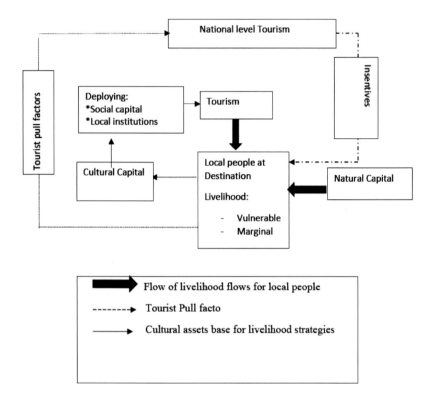

Figure 6.1: Incentive-based cultural tourism options

6.4   Future research

Further study may focus to understand more of the unevenly distributed little gains among the local people observed in the QOL survey in terms of who gains most and why.

References

Abbink, G.J. (2002). Tourism and its discontents: Suri-tourist encounters in southern Ethiopia. *Journal of Social Anthropology*. 8 (1) 1 – 17.

Abbink, Jon. 2009. "Suri Images: The Return of Exoticism and the Commodification of an Ethiopian 'Tribe'." *Cachiers d'Etudes Africaines XLIX (4):893-924.*

Abebe, T. (2019). Reconceptualizing Children's Agency as Continuum and Interdependence. *Soc. Sci.* **2019**, *8*, 81.

Adams, W. M., & Hutton, J. (2007). People, Parks and Poverty. *Political Ecology and Biodiversity Conservation.* 5(2), 147–183.

Ali Y (2016) Challenge and Prospect of Ethiopian Tourism Policy. *Journal of Hotel and Business Management* 5: 134.

Aref, F. (2011). The effect of Tourism on Quality of Life. A case study of Shiraz. Iran. *Life science journal.* 8(2). 27-36.

Ashley, C. (200b). The Impact of Tourism on Rural Livelihoods: Namibia's Experience, London: Overseas Development Institute.

Assefa Fanta and Derege Ayalew (2019) Status and control measures of fall armyworm (Spodoptera Frugiperda) infestation in maize fields in Ethiopia. A review. *Cogen food and agriculture 5:1.*

Agarawala, M., Atkinson, G., Fry, B. P., Homewood, K., Mourato, S., Rowcliffe, J. M., Wallace, G., and Milner-Gulland, E. J. (2014). Assessing the relationship between human well-being and ecosystem services: a review of frameworks. Conservation and Society, 12(4), 437-449

Bebbington, A. (1999). Capitals and Capabilities: A Framework for Analyzing peasant viability. Rural Livelihoods and Poverty. World Development, 27, 2021-2034.

Blaikie, P., Cannon, T., Davis, I. and Wisner, B. (1994). *At risk, Natural hazards, people's vulnerability and disasters*. London. Routledge.

Bourdieu, P. (1986). "The Forms of Capital. In J. G. Richardson. *Handbook of Theory and Research for the Sociology of Education* (Pp. 241-258). New York. Greenwood Press.

Buckingham, D. (2009). Creative visual methods in Media research: Possibilities, problems and proposals. *Media, culture & society. 31 (4): 633-652.*

Burns, P.M. (1999). *An Introduction to tourism and anthropology*. Psychology Press.

Burns, P.M. (2008). Tourism, political discourse, and post-colonialism. *Tourism and Hospitality Planning & Development*, 5(1), 61-71.

Butterworth, J.; Sutton, S. and Mecosta, L. (2013). Self-supply as a complementary water services delivery model in Ethiopia. *Water Alternatives 6(3): 405-423.*

Camfield, L., G. Crivello and M. Woodlhead (2009). Wellbeing research in developing countries: Reviewing the role of qualitative methods. *Social Indicators Research,* 90(1): 5-31.

Chambers, R., &   Conway, G. (1992*). Sustainable rural livelihoods: Practical concepts for the 21ˢᵗ century.* Institute of Development Sutdies (UK).

Chambers R. (2008). *Revolutions in development inquiry.* USA. Earthscan.

Cohen, E. (1988) Authenticity and commoditization in tourism. *Annals of Tourism Research* 15(3):371-386.

CSA (2008a). *Summary and statistical report of the 2007 population and housing census: population size by age and sex, Federal Democratic Republic of Ethiopia.* Population Census Commission, with support from UNFPA.

CSA (2008b). *The 2007 population and housing census of Ethiopia: statistical report for Southern Nations, Nationalities and People`s Region.* Addis Ababa, Ethiopia.

Cummins, R. A. (1996). *Assessing quality of life. In R. I. Brown (Ed.)* Quality of Life for Handicapped People, Chapman & Hall: London

Cummins, R. A. (1997). The domain of life satisfaction: an attempt to order chaos. *Social Indicator Research*, 38, 303-0328.

Davis, S. (1996). *Adaptable Livelihoods: Coping with Food Insecurity in the Malian Sahel.* London: Macmillan Press.

De Haan. L. J. (2012). *The Livelihood approach: A critical exploration.* Erdkunde, 345-357.

Dodds, R., Alisha, A., and Galaski, K. (2016). Mobilizing Knowledge: Determining key elements for success and pitfalls in developing Community Based tourism. *Current Issues in Tourism*, 21 (13), 1547-1568.

Dodge, R., Daly, A. P., Huyton, J., & Sanders, L. D. (2012). The challenge of defining wellbeing. *2*, 222–235.

Dorfman, D and Northwest Regional Educational Lab., Portland, OR, Rural Education Program. (1998). Mapping Community Assets Workbook. Strengthening Community Education: The Basis for Sustainable Renewal. [Washington D.C.]: Distributed by ERIC Clearninghouse, htt@s://eric.ed.gove/?id=ED426499

Edwards, D., (2004). *Art Therapy. London,* Sage Publications.

Elder, Glen H Jr, Monica K. J., and Crosnoe.R.(2003). *The emergence and development of life course theory.* in T, Jeylan, J. Mortimer and J. Michael Shanahan (Ed). Handbook of the Life Course, (Pp. 3-19) New York. Kluwer Academic/ Plenum Publlshers.

Ellis, F. (2000). *Rural Livelihoods and Diversity in developing countries.* University press, Oxford

Ethiopian Wildlife Conservation Authority (2011). *Existing challenge: Plantation Development versus wildlife conservation in the Omo-Tama-Mago complex*. Report.

Enyew BD, Hutjis R (2015). Climate Change Impact and Adaptation in SOZ, Ethiopia. Journal of Geology & Geophysics, *4:208.*

Endashaw Terefe, Tadelle Dessie, Aynalem Haile, Wudyalew Mulatu and Okeyo Mwai, (2012). Husbandry and breeding practices of cattle in Mursi and Bodi pastoral communities in Southwest Ethiopia. *African Journal of Agricultural Research,* 7 (45), 5986-5994.

EU Emergency Trust Fund of Africa (2016). *Cross-Border Analysis and Mapping. Cluster 1: Southwest Ethiopia-Northwest Kenya.* Final Report.

Federal Democratic Republic of Ethiopia. (2016). *Growth and Transformation Plan II (GTP II), (2015/16-2019/20). Volume I.* Main Text. National Planning Commission. Addis Ababa.

Freeman, D. and Pankhurst, A. (2001). *Living on the Edge: Marginalized Minorities of Craftworkers and hunters in Southern Ethiopia.* Addis Ababa: Addis Ababa University, College of Social Sciences.

Gauntlett D & Holzwarth P. (2006). Creative and visual methods for exploring identities. *Visual Studies, 21 (1):82-91.*

Gebre, Y. (2016). Reality Checks: The state of civil society organizations in Ethiopia. *African Sociological Review / Revue Africaine De Sociologie, 20*(2), 2-25. Retrieved from www.jstor.org/stable/90001853

Gillian F. Black, Alun Davies, Dalia Iskander & Mary Chambers (2018). Reflections on the ethics of participatory visual methods to engage communities in global health research, *Global Bioethics, 29:1, 22-38*

Glow, X., Indre, K., Kable, A., Hazelton, M., (2017). Visual Methodologies in Qualitative Research Autophotography and Photo Elicitation Applied to Mental Health Research. *International journal of qualitative method, Vol. 16:1-8.*

Goodwin, H., Santilli R. (2009). *Community-based Tourism a Success?* Report. German Development Agency (GTZ).

Gomez, M., Medina, F. X., and Arilla. J. M. P. (2016). New trends in tourism? From globalization to postmodernism. *International journal of scientific management and touris,* 2(3), 417-433.

Greenwood, D. (1977). Culture by the Pound: Anthropological perspective on tourism as culture commoditization. In V. L. Smith (Ed.). In   Hosts and Guests (pp. 129138). Philadelphia: University of Pennsylvania Press.

Hall, C.M. and Tucker, H. (eds) (2004). *Tourism and Post-colonialism: Contested Discourses, Identities and Representations.* New York & London: Routledge.

Haan, L. De, & Zoomers, A. (2005). Exploring the Frontier of Livelihoods Research. *Development and Change, 36(1), 27–47: 27-47*

Harrison D. (ed) (1992). *Tourism and the Less Developed Countries*. London. D. Belhaven Press.

Hitlin, Steven, and Glen H Jr Elder. 2006. Agency: An empirical model of an abstract concept. *Advances in life course research, 11:33-67.*

Hitlin S. and Elder G H. (2007). Time, Self, and the Curiously Abstract Concept of Agency. *Sociological Theory,* 25(2):170-91.

Holden A. Scoones, J. and Novelli, (2011). Tourism and Poverty Reduction: An Interpretation by the Poor of Elmina, Ghana, Tourism Planning & Development, 3:3, 317–334

Kaneko, Morie, (2005). *Transmigration among* Aari *Women Potters in Southwestern Ethiopia and the Accumulation of Experience in Pottery-Making Techniques.* African study monographs. Suppl., 46:27-52

Lambert, J. (2013). *Digital Storytelling: Capturing lives, creating community.* 4th edition. NY, Routledge.

LaToysky, S. (2013). *Predicaments of Mursi (Mun) Women in Ethiopia's Changing World. Germany.* Klever GmbH, Bergishch Gladbach.

Lea, J.(1988). *Tourism and development in the Third World. Methuen Introductions to Development.* London: Routledge.

Lewis, D. (2005). Anthropology and development: the uneasy relationship [online]. London: LSE   Research   Online.   Available at :http://eprints.lse.ac.uk/archive/00000253

Leiper, N. (1979). The framework of tourism: Towards a definition of tourism, tourist, and the tourist industry. Annals of tourism research, 6(4), 390-407.

Lightfoot, E., Mccleary, J. S., & Lum, T. (2014). Asset Mapping as a Research Tool for community-Based Paricipator Research in Social work. *Soial work research, 38(1): 59–64.*

MacCannell, D. (1973). Staged Authenticity: Arrangements of Social Space in Tourist Settings, *American Journal of Sociology, 79, no. 3 (Nov. 1973): 589-603.*

MacCannell, D. (1999). *The Tourist: A new Theory of the Leisure Class.* University of California Press, Berkley, Los Angeles, London.

Manlosa, A. O. (2019). Livelihood strategies , capital assets , and food security in rural Southwest Ethiopia. *Food Security, 11:167–181.*

Mitchell, J. and Ashley, C. (2010). *Tourism and Poverty Reduction. Pathway to Prosperity.* London: Earthscan.

Mihalic, T. (2014). Tourism and Economic Development Issues. In R. Sharpley & D. Telfer,

J. (Eds.), Tourism and Development. Concepts and Issues. (2nd ed., pp. 77-117). Toronto: Channel View Publications.

Moscardo, G. (2008). Sustainable tourism innovation : Challenging. *Tourism and Hospitality Research*, 8(1), 4–13.

Naty, A. (1978). Memory and the Humiliation of Men: The revolution in Aari. In W. James, D. L. Donham, E. Kurimoto, and A. Trilzi (eds.) Oxford. James Currey Publishers. Pp.59-73.

Nash D., Akeroid, A. V., Bodine, J.J., Cohen, E., Dann, G., Graburne, N. H., D. (1981). Tourism as an anthropological subject [and comments and reply]. Current anthropology, 22 (5), 461-481.

Nash, D. (1996). *Anthropology of tourism.* Pergamon. New York.

Netherlands Ministry of Foreign Affairs (2018). Analysis of tourism value chain in Ethiopia. Final Report. Center for promotion of Imports (CBI).

Nishizaki, N (2014). Neoliberal Conservation in Ethiopia: An Analysis of Current Conflicts in and Around Protected Areas and their Resolution. *African Study Monographs, Suppl.* 50: 191–205.

Nishizaki, N. (2019). 'An Ethiopian Alternative to "Traditional" Ethnic Tourism'. *Global-e. Twenty-first Century Global Dynamics.* Thursday January, 2019. https://www.21global.ucsb.edu/global-e/january-2019/ethiopian-alternative-traditiona l-ethnic-tourism (Accessed 22 May, 2019).

Novelli M. (2016). *Tourism and Development in Sub-Saharan Africa.* Current issues and local realities. New York, Routledge

Ochieng NT, Wilson K, Derrick CJ, Mukherjee N. (2018). The use of focus group discussion methodology: Insights from two decades of application in conservation. *Methods in Ecology and Evolution.* 9:20–32.

Regi, T. (2012). Tourism, leisure and work in an east African pastoral society. *Anthropology Today. Vol. 28 No. 5,*

Regi, T. (2013). The art of the weak: Tourist encounter in East Africa. *Tourist Studies.13(1) 99 – 118.*

Regi, T. (2014). The anthropology of tourism and development in Africa: mobile identities in a   pastoral society in South-Ethiopia'. , *Int. J. Tourism Anthropology,* 3 (4), 302- 324.

Richards, G. (2018). Cultural tourism: A review of recent research and trends. *Journal of Hospitality and Tourism management 36 – 12-21.*

Rose, G. (2012). *Visual Methodologies: An introduction to researching with visual materials.* 3rd edition. London. Sage publications.

Rowlands, J. (1997). Questioning women's empowerment: working with women in

Honduras. Oxford.

Scarles, C. (2012). The Photographed Other: Interplays of Agency in Tourist Photography in Cusco, Peru. *Annals of Tourism Research, 39*(2), 928–950.

Scoones, I. (1998) Sustainable Rural Livelihoods: A Framework for Analysis, IDS Working Paper 72, Brighton: IDS.

Sharpley R. & Telfer D. (Eds) (2015). *Tourism and Development. Concepts and Issues. 2ⁿᵈ* edition. Bristol. Channel View Publishers.

Shaw, J. (2012). Beyond Empowerment Inspiration: Interrogating the Gap between the Ideals and Practice Reality of Participatory Video in E. J. Milne, C. Mitchell, and N. de Lange (eds.) Handbook of Participatory Video Altamira Press.

Shigeta, Masayoshi. (1990). Folk in Situ Conservation of Ensete [Ensete ventricosum (Welw) E.E. Cheesman]: Toward the interpretation of indigenous Agricultural Science of the Ari, Southwestern Ethiopia. *Asia Africa Area Studies. 2*

Smith, Valene L (1989). *Hosts and guests: the anthropology of tourism* (2nd ed). Philadelphia, University of Pennsylvania Press,

Smith, M., K. (2014). *Issues in Cultural Tourism Studies.* London. Routledge.

Sontag, S. (1979). *On photography.* Harmondsworth: Penguin Books.

Sirgy M. I. (2002). *The psychology of quality of life.* Dordrecht, the Netherlands, Kluwer Academic.

Stiglitz, J., Sen, A., & Fitoussi, J.P. (2009). The measurement of economic performance and social progress revisited. Reflections and overview. Commission on the measurement of economic performance and social progress, Paris.

Strecker Y. (2014). In Mulugeta G.B. (2014). *A Delicate Balance. Land use, Minority Rights and Social Stability in the Horn of Africa.* Institute for Peace and Security Studies. Addis Ababa University.

Sontag, S. (1979) *On photography.* Harmondsworth: Penguin Books.

Sullivan, G. M., & Artino, A. R., Jr (2013). Analyzing and interpreting data from likert-type scales. *Journal of graduate medical education, 5*(4), 541–542.

Suryabhava K.V. (2017). GIS-based climate variability and drought characteristics in Ethiopia over three decades. Weather and climate Extremes. 15:11-23.

Tadesse, Barisso (1995). *Agricultural and rural development policies in Ethiopia: a case study of villagization policy among the Guji-Oromo of Jama Jama Awraja.* Michigan State University PhD Dissertation.

Terefe E., Dessie, T,m Haile, A. Mulatu, W., & Mwai, O. (2012). Husbandry and breeding practices of cattle in Mursi and Bodi pastoral communities in Southwest Ethiopia.

African *Journal of Agricultural Research,* 7(45), 5986-5994.

Telfer, D., Sharpley, R. (2008). *Tourism and Development in the Developing World.* London: Routledge,

Tomaselli, K. G. (Ed.). (2012). *Cultural tourism and identity: Rethinking indigeneity.* Leiden: Martinus Nijhoff Pbulishers.

Tewolde Woldemariam and Fana Gebresenbet. (2014). *In Mulugeta G.B. A Delicate Balance. Land use, Minority Rights and Social Stability in the Horn of Africa. Institute for Peace and Security Studies.* Addis Ababa University.

Throsby, D. (2001). *Economics and Culture.* Cambridge: Cambridge University Press.

Throsby, D. (1999). Cultural Capital. *Journal of Cultural Economics 23 (1):3-12*

Turner, L., Ash, J., (1975). *The Golden Hordes: International tourism and the Pleasure Periphery.* USA. University of Michigan.

Turton, D. (1978). Territorial Organization and Age among the Mursi, in P.T.W. Baxter & U.   Almagor (eds.) *Age, Generation and Time: Some Features of East African Age Organizations,* Hurst, London, pp. 95-130.

Turton, D. (1979). A journey made them: territorial segmentation and ethnic identity among the Mursi', In n L. Holy (ed.), *Segmentary lineage systems reconsidered.* Department of Social Anthropology. Volume 4, (pp. 119-43,), Belfast. Queen's University

Turton, D. (1981). Exploration in the Lower Omo Valley of Southwesterrn Ethiopia between 1890 and 1910. In (M. Caravaglios, ed) L'Africa ai Tempi di Daniele Comboni; pp. 1-10. Istituto Italo-Africano, Rome.

Turton, D. (1985). Mursi resonse to drought: Some lessons for relief and rehabilitation. African Affairs, 84(336): 331-346.

Turton D. (1988). Looking for a cool place: the Mursi, 1890s-1990s. In D. Anderson and D. Johnson (eds.). The Ecology of Survival: Case Studies from Northeast African History (pp. 261 – 82). London/Boulder. Westview Press.

Turton, D. (1995). Pastoral Livelihoods in Danger: Cattle Disease, Drought, and Wildlife Conservation in Mursiland, South-Western Ethio@ia. Oxfam Publications, Oxford.

Turton, D., (2002). The Mursi and the Elephant Question. In (D. Chatty & M. Colchester eds.) Conservation and Mobile Indigenous Peoples: *Displacement, Forced Settlement and development*, pp. 97-118. Berghahn Books, Oxford and New York.

Turton, D. (2004). Lip-plates and the people who take photographs. Unease encounters between Mursi and Toruists in South Ethiopia. *Anthropology Today* vol. 20 (3) 3-8.

Turton, D. (2005). The meaning of place in a world of movement: Lessons from long-term field research in Southern Ethiopia. *Journal of Refugee Studies, 18*(3), 258–280.

Turton, D (2013). *Aiding and Abetting: UK and US Complicity in Ethiopia's Mass Displacement.* Online. https://web.archive.org/web/2014112513806; http://thinkafrica press.com/Ethiopia/politics-stupid-ukaid-and-and-human-rights-abuses-lower-omo-va lley(Accessed May 16,2019).

UN General Assembly (2015). *Transforming our world: the 2030 Agenda for Sustainable Development*, 21 October 2015.

UNECA. (2015). *The Federal Democratic Republic of Ethiopia. Sustainable Tourism Master Plan* 2015-2025. Ministry of Culture and Tourism.

Urry, J. (1999). *Sensing leisure spaces. In Crouch, D. (ed.) Leisure/Tourism Geographies: Practices and Geographical Knowledge, London: Routledge, pp. 34-45.*

Uysal, M., Sirgy, M. J., Woo, E., & Kim, H. L. (2016). Quality of life (QOL) and well-being research in tourism. *Tourism Management*, *53*, 244-261.

Walsh, S. (2012). Challenging knowledge production with participatory video. *In E J Milne, C Mitchell, and N de Lange (eds.) Handbook of Participatory Video.* Lanham MD: Altamira Press pp. 242-256.

Whoqol Group. (1998). Development of the World Health Organization WHOQOL-BREF quality of life assessment. *Psychological medicine*, *28*(3), 551-558.

Woo, E., Kim, H., Uysal, M. (2015). Life satisfaction and support for tourism development. *Annals of tourism Research*, 50, 84-97.

World Bank (2006) *Towards a Strategy for Pro-Poor Tourism Development.* Prepared for the Government of Ethiopia.

World Tourism Organization (2011). *UNWTO Annual Report 2010, UNWTO, Mardrid,* DOI: https://dx.doi.org/10.18111/9789284415359

World Tourism Organization (1980). Manila Declaration on World Tourism, UNWTO Declarations, volume 1, number 1, UNWTO, Madrid, DOI: https://doi.org/10.18111/unwtodeclarations.1980.01.01

Annex

Annex 1

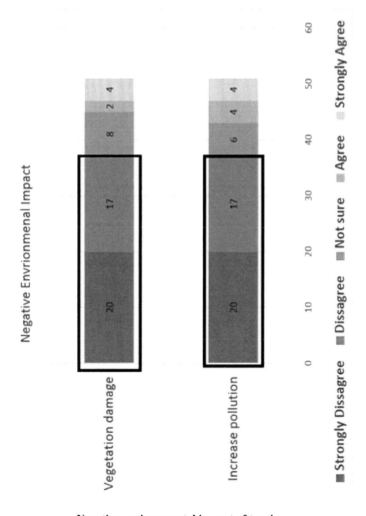

Negative environmental impact of tourism

Annex 2

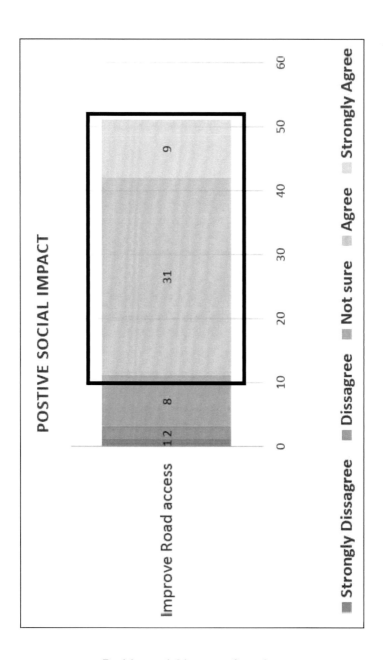

Positive social impact of tourism

Annex 3

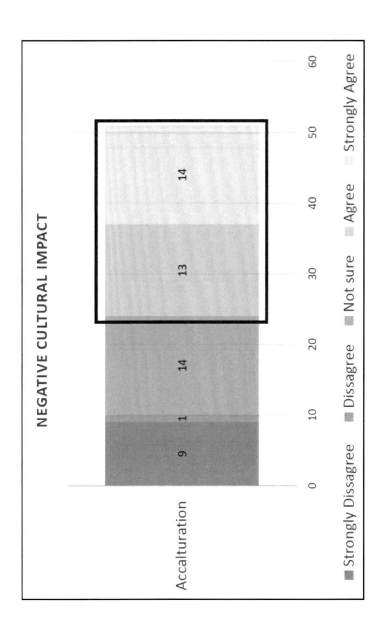

Negative environmental impact of tourism

Annex 4

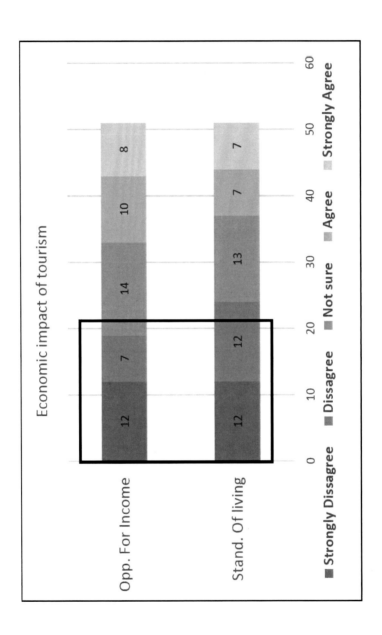

Economic impact of tourism

Annex 5

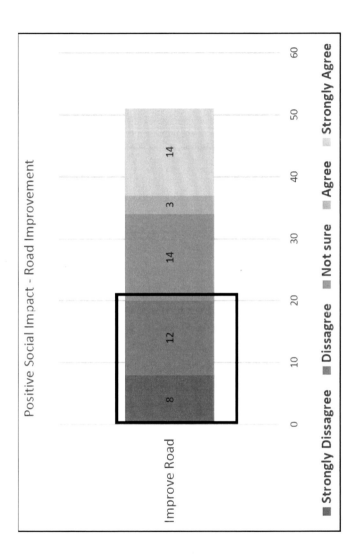

Positive social impact – Road improvement

Annex 6

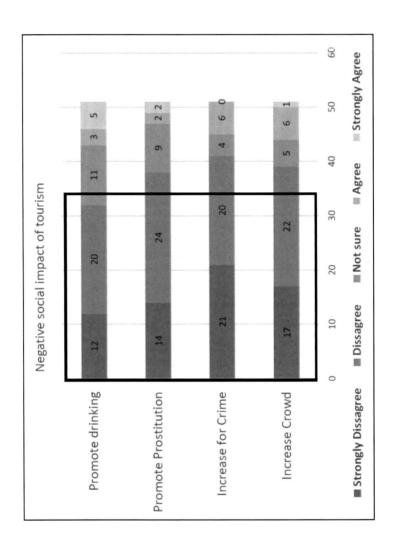

Negative social impact of tourism

Annex 7

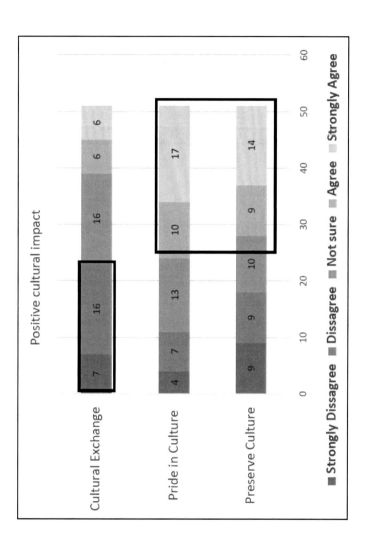

Positive cultural impact of tourism

Annex 8

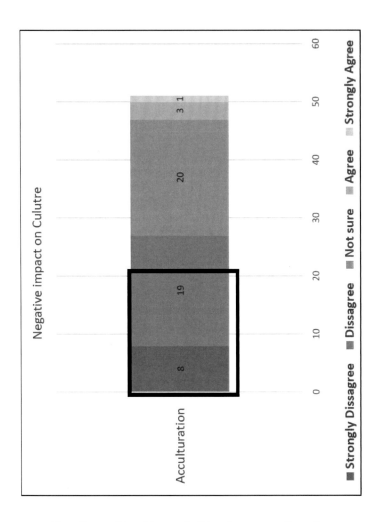

Negative cultural impact of tourism - acculturation

Annex 9

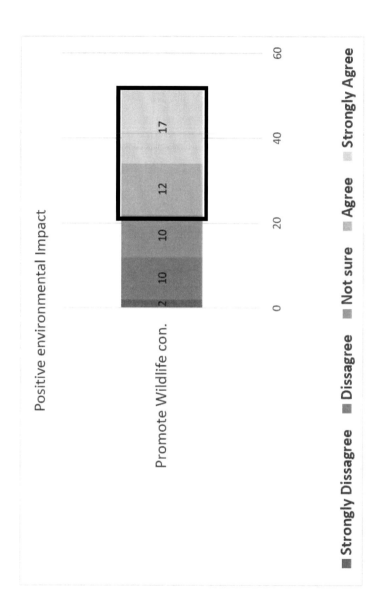

Positive environmental impact of tourism - Promote wildlife conservation

Annex 10

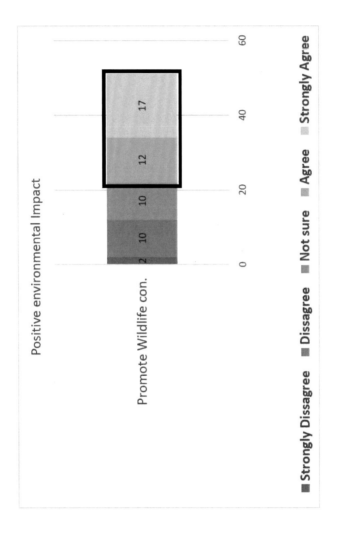

Positive environmental impact of tourism - Promote wildlife conservation

Annex 11

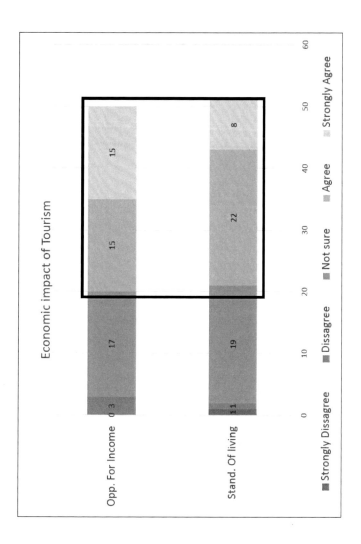

Economic impact of tourism in Mursiland

Annex 12

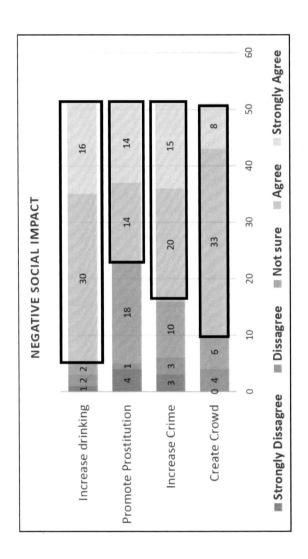

Negative social impact of tourism

Annex 13

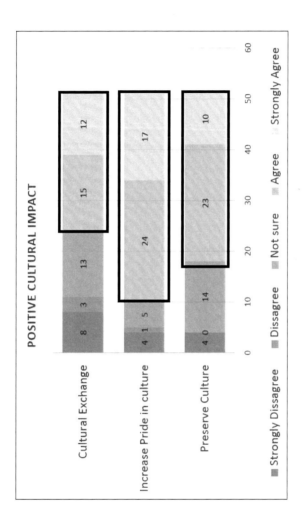

Positive cultural impact of tourism

Annex 14

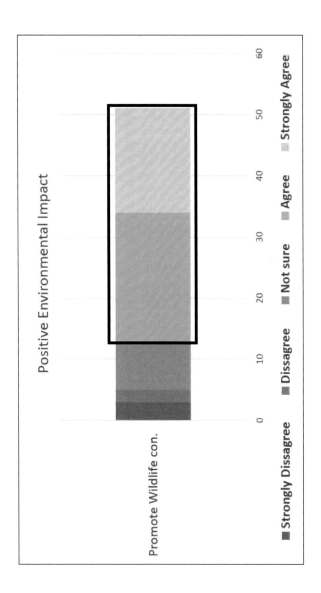

Positive environmental impact of tourism

Annex 15

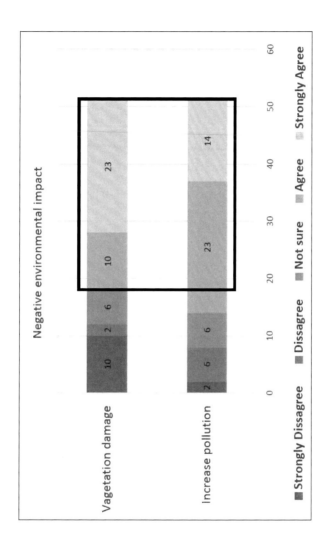

Negative environmental impact of tourism

Annex 16

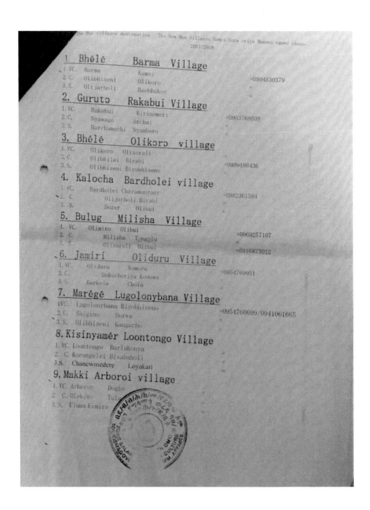

Zonal letter to guide associations on request of Mursi local people

Annex 17

Jinka/Yetnebersh QOL survey session

Annex 18

Mursi Likert Scale survey session

Annex 19

Exhibition poster

Annex 20

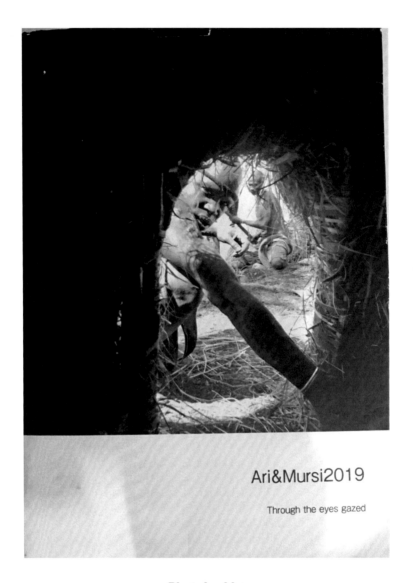

Ari&Mursi2019

Through the eyes gazed

Photo booklet

Annex 21

Exhibition session – Jinka University

Annex 22

Focus group discussion participants, February 2019

Annex 23

Event of Exhibition, Jinka University

Annex 24

Concept/ English Amharic	In Mursi	In Ari
Life/ Nuro	Babaga – Shumunugne	Hanbish dokintin usto
Local facility/ mesertc limat	Babaga	Dokinti
Basic needs (food, housing, clothing)	Tila, dori, rum	Atmi, ay, Abla
Income	Aha Kojowana	Abintigogi
School/education/ Timirt bet	Doria timirtiygn/ timirti	Abintigogi
Community/neighborhood life	Hinenina-baygne	Edki Kin Dokintin Usto
Security Dehninet/tsetita	Ba chalin	Lekmi (dehninet)
Recreation/Leisure time/ meznanat zize	Tirign	
Spiritural life Menfesawi hiwot/ Emnet hiwot	Yewa	Emnet
Culture/Bahil	Goto	Karta (fechenta kharta – yeager bahil)
Safety dehninet	Re challin)	Lekmi mato
Health/tenegna/tena	Hinenine	teninet
Water/ wiha/ye wiha tirat/nitsihna	Ma	Noka
Crowded / Mechenanek	Shura	mechenanek
Crime/wenjel	Tukuri-noi (later corrected by community as - Hume)	Dekli-woni
Prosititution/ Zimut	Lolumo	zimut
Drinking/techy mehon/sikar	Drink – Matinen Drankness - luti	Drink – wochni Sikar - gogi
Improvement/meshashal	Loga kachcha ke challi	lewitsmeto
Pride / mekurat	Eran	Kori
Adulterate/meberez	Goto-basayi	Bukui
Cultural exchange/ yebahil liwiwit	Goto-Chacha	Kartem kik dank esinti
Pollution/Biklet	HaHa Udu	Dakli
Wild animals	Aha Gashungn	Kaw-te-debi

Translation on selected concepts to elaborate questionnaires

Publication of the Kyoto University Africa Studies Research Series

The Center for African Area Studies at Kyoto University is a research institution whose precursor was founded in 1986 as the first comprehensive research institution covering Africa. Since its establishment, the institution has been known as the Africa Center, a base for academic research into the African region. Contemporary Africa is currently undergoing significant change in all aspects, be they environmental, social, cultural, political, or economic. It is through that the status of Africa and the role it plays on the world stage will become increasingly important in the future. We are in era where Africa's fundamental purpose is being questioned on multiple forms, and we should look toward Africa and understand it as a place inhabited by those of the same era as ourselves as we continue to study it. With this desire at heart, Kyoto University continues to produce young scholars researching Africa. This series aims to present the wider public with the rigorous fieldwork and groundbreaking analysis being conducted by a new wave of ambitious young researchers and was initiated with the support of the 2010 Kyoto University President's Discretionary Fund (Assistance to Publish Young Research) to mark the 25th anniversary of the establishment of the Africa Center.

February 2011
The Center for African Area Studies, Kyoto University

Azeb Girmai

Azeb Girmai is a researcher. Born in Addis Ababa Ethiopia. She accomplished her Honors Bachelor of Arts, in 1996 at the East London University, UK. Since 1997, for over 15 years she worked in the NGO sector as development practitioner, particularly with a special focus on the synergy of development and environmental interventions in Ethiopia. In 2013 she obtained her Master of Science degree from the Center for Development, Environment and Policy, SOAS, University of London. Consecutively, she joined LDC Watch International to advocate for climate change policy issues in Africa Least Developed Countries until 2016. In 2017 joining the Graduate School of Asian and African Area Studies, she researched on the significance of Cultural Tourism on local Livelihoods and Wellbeing in the Lower Omo Valley, Southwestern Ethiopia and accomplished her Doctor of Areas studies degree in 2020.

京都大学アフリカ研究シリーズ 028

Cultural tourism potentials towards livelihood security:
Local perceptions in Southern Ethiopia

2021 年 3 月 30 日　初版発行
著者　Azeb Girmai
発行者 松香堂書店
発行所　京都大学アフリカ地域研究資料センター
〒606-8501　京都市左京区吉田下阿達町46
TEL : 075-753-7800
Email : caas@jambo.africa.kyoto-u.ac.jp